More Earth Science Titles in the Inquire & Investigate Series

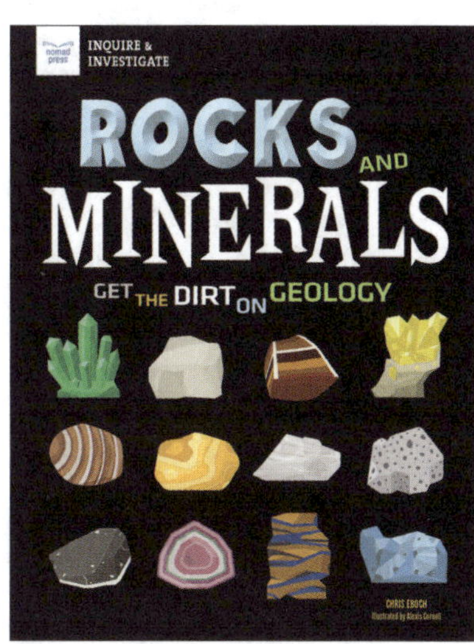

You can use a smartphone or tablet app to scan the QR codes and explore more! Cover up neighboring QR codes to make sure you're scanning the right one. You can find a list of URLs on the Resources page.

If the QR code doesn't work, try searching the internet with the Keyword Prompts to find other helpful sources.

climate change

CLIMATE IN CRISIS

CHANGING COASTLINES, SEVERE STORMS, AND DAMAGING DROUGHT

Carla Mooney

Illustrated by Traci Van Wagoner

Nomad Press

A division of Nomad Communications

10 9 8 7 6 5 4 3 2 1

This book was manufactured by Versa Press,
East Peoria, Illinois, United States
April 2022, Job #J21-5442

ISBN Softcover: 978-1-64741-064-3
ISBN Hardcover: 978-1-64741-061-2

Educational Consultant, Marla Conn

Questions regarding the ordering of this book should be addressed to
Nomad Press
PO Box 1036, Norwich, VT 05055
www.nomadpress.net

Printed in the United States.

Contents

TIMELINE

1827: French scientist Jean-Baptiste Fourier uses a greenhouse analogy to predict global warming.

1863: Irish scientist John Tyndall describes water vapor as a greenhouse gas.

1890s: Swedish scientist Svante Arrhenius calculates that burning fossil fuels could lead to the buildup of carbon dioxide in the atmosphere and global warming.

1890s to 1940: Earth's average surface air temperatures rise by about 0.25 degrees Celsius.

1940 to 1970: Earth's average temperatures cool about 0.2 degrees Celsius. Scientists begin to lose interest in greenhouse gas effects.

1957: American oceanographer David Keeling sets up the first continuous monitoring of carbon dioxide levels in the atmosphere.

1960: Keeling accurately measures carbon dioxide in the Earth's atmosphere and detects a yearly rise.

1970s: Gasoline shortages spark renewed interest in electric cars.

1980s: The coldest years in the 1980s are warmer than the warmest years a century earlier.

1988: The United Nations creates the Intergovernmental Panel on Climate Change (IPCC) to analyze and report on the scientific study of climate change.

1990: The IPCC finds that Earth has warmed by 0.5 degrees Celsius during the last 100 years. It warns that strong measures are needed to slow greenhouse gas emissions and prevent serious climate change.

1992: The United Nations creates the UN Framework Convention on Climate Change. The Climate Change Convention is signed by 154 countries with an initial target of lowering greenhouse gas emissions from industrialized countries to 1990 levels by 2000.

1997: The Kyoto Protocol, signed by 192 countries, commits industrialized countries and economies in transition to limit and reduce greenhouse gases emissions in accordance with agreed individual targets. The Toyota Prius is released in Japan and becomes the world's first mass-produced hybrid electric vehicle.

2002: In Earth's second-hottest year on record, Antarctica's Larsen B ice sheet breaks up.

2003: Europe experiences the hottest summer in at least 500 years. About 30,000 people die from the extreme heat.

2006: Researchers discover that carbon dioxide emissions are rising faster than they did during the 1990s.

2008: The polar bear is listed as an endangered species because of the risk to its habitat from climate change. Thousands of species are threatened by climate change.

2015: The Paris Agreement, an international treaty on climate change, replaces the Kyoto Protocol. Its goal is to hold global temperature rise to below 2 degrees Celsius and cut net greenhouse gas emissions to zero by mid-century. Nearly 200 countries, including the United States, sign the Paris Agreement.

2018: An IPCC report states that Earth's greenhouse gas emissions must significantly decline by 2030 to avoid disastrous warming.

2019: Costa Rica generates 98 percent of its energy from renewable resources for the fifth straight year.

2020: The U.S. Congress passes a stimulus bill that includes an agreement to phase out hydrofluorocarbons, chemicals used in refrigeration and air conditioning that contribute to global warming.

2021: Historic heat, drought, wildfires, flooding, and storms devastate communities worldwide. World leaders at the COP26 global climate conference in Glasgow, Scotland, pledge to stop deforestation and cut methane emissions to slow climate change.

climate
diverse
climate change
weather
activism
atmosphere
carbon dioxide
ecosystem
climatologist
endangered
conserve
pollutant
water vapor
water cycle
extinction
deforestation
adapt
anxiety
drought
chemistry
coral bleaching
hectare
energy
biofuel
greenhouse effect
flash flood
coral reef
erosion
dense
diabetes
high tide
greenhouse gases
fossil fuels
savannah
dioxide
succulent
emissions
global
dehydration
heatstroke
humidity
wildfire
runoff
vitamin
acidic

Introduction

Our Changing Climate

What makes today's climate change different from climate change in the past?

Scientists recognize that the climate change we see today is caused primarily by human activity. We use lots of energy in our daily lives and that energy has a cost—the increase of greenhouse gases in our atmosphere, which is leading to a rapidly changing global climate.

In 2018, a 15-year-old Swedish student named Greta Thunberg (2003–) became famous when she skipped school to protest climate change. After witnessing a summer of wildfires and heatwaves in her country, Thunberg grew increasingly concerned about the impact of climate change on the earth and everyone who lives on it. She was infuriated that the adults in charge appeared to be doing very little to slow or stop climate change.

Thunberg decided to take action.

She went to the Swedish parliament to protest. She held a sign that said, "School Strike for Climate," in Swedish. At the time, she was one girl, standing alone to bring attention to climate change.

News of Thunberg's activism quickly spread around the world. Thunberg's passion for creating awareness about Earth's changing climate was easy to see, despite her young age.

She argued that young people would suffer the most if world leaders did not do something immediately to address climate change. She also pointed out that climate change was no longer a problem that could be pushed off until the future. Living creatures in certain parts of the world were already suffering from the effects of climate change. Thunberg's message resonated with millions of adults and young people. During the following weeks and months, many people joined her and organized climate strikes in countries worldwide.

As her recognition grew, Thunberg was invited to speak at numerous global climate change events. At the 2019 World Economic Forum in Switzerland, she warned the audience that, "Our house is on fire."

Thunberg attends the 2019 European Economic and Social Committee event in Brussels, Belgium.

> "We are facing a disaster of unspoken suffering for enormous amounts of people. And now is not the time for speaking politely or focusing on what we can or cannot say. Now is the time to speak clearly. Solving the climate crisis is the greatest and most complex challenge that *Homo sapiens* has ever faced."

She urged the audience to take action against climate change. Today, Thunberg continues to work tirelessly to make a difference in the world and raise awareness about climate change.

PRIMARY SOURCES

Primary sources come from people who were eyewitnesses to events. They might write about the event, take pictures, post short messages to social media or blogs, or record the event for radio or video. The photographs in this book are primary sources, taken at the time of the event. Paintings of events are usually not primary sources, since they were often painted long after the event took place. What other primary sources can you find? Why are primary sources important? Do you learn differently from primary sources than from secondary sources, which come from people who did not directly experience the event?

Watch Greta Thunberg give her "Our House Is on Fire" speech at the World Economic Forum 2019.

Why is it important for young people to speak out on topics such as climate change? How might their perspectives be different from those of older people?

Thunberg house fire

AN IMPORTANT TOPIC

Climate change is all over the news. Activists such as Greta Thunberg organize protests and events to raise awareness about climate change. Scientists talk about global warming, greenhouse gases, and the ozone layer. Sometimes, all of the technical jargon can make climate change seem overwhelming and confusing. What is climate change? What causes it? And why is climate change important to you?

You've probably already experienced some of the effects of climate change firsthand, without even knowing it. Have you noticed that seasons feel different from year to year? Does your region get stronger storms and more extreme weather than it used to? Do you have to take steps to conserve water because of drought? Is there more flooding in your area than there used to be? Are some local birds and other animals disappearing? Do you notice new plants taking over in some places?

All of these could be signs of Earth's climate crisis.

CLIMATE VS. WEATHER

Before we dive into all of the ways climate change affects you and your fellow humans, let's first take a look at the difference between weather and climate.

Weather is what happens in the atmosphere every day.

Is it rainy or sunny outside? Is the temperature hot or cold? Weather can change minute to minute, hour to hour, and day by day. For example, it might be sunny in the morning and raining in the afternoon in your neighborhood. Weather also varies in different places in the world. On any given day, the weather in Florida is often different from the weather in Alaska. Most weather occurs in the troposphere, which is the part of Earth's atmosphere closest to Earth's surface.

Climate, on the other hand, means the usual weather or weather pattern of an area. Climate can vary from place to place. For example, Arizona's climate is typically hot and dry. Seattle's climate tends to be cooler and wetter. Climate can also vary by season in the same place. Your town might be hot and humid in the summer months and cold and snowy in the winter.

Planet Earth also has a climate. Earth's climate is the combination of all the climates around the world. If Earth's global climate changes, regional climates also change. This changes the weather, too. For example, as Earth's climate warms, scientists predict more hot summer days in many regions and fewer frigid days.

CLIMATE CLUES

Scientists use satellites and surface instruments to monitor the natural events and human activities that affect climate.

SCIENTIFIC METHOD

The scientific method is the process scientists use to ask questions and find answers. Keep a science journal to record your methods and observations during all the activities in this book. You can use a scientific method worksheet to keep your ideas and observations organized.

Question: What are we trying to find out? What problem are we trying to solve?

Research: What is already known about this topic?

Hypothesis: What do we think the answer will be?

Equipment: What supplies are we using?

Method: What procedure are we following?

Results: What happened and why?

WHAT IS CLIMATE CHANGE?

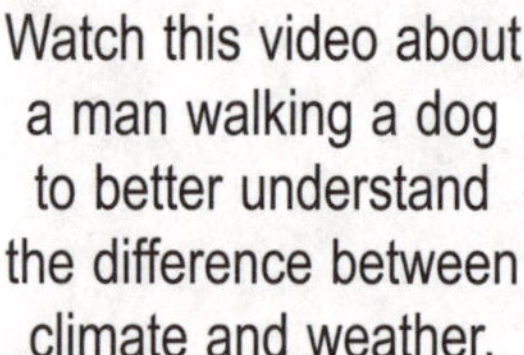

Watch this video about a man walking a dog to better understand the difference between climate and weather.

What are some other images that can be used to show this phenomenon?

weather climate dog

When a region's usual weather changes through time, that can be a sign of climate change. Some of those changes might include average temperatures, the amount of rainfall, and the intensity of storms in that area. While weather changes day to day, climate change is slower. It can take hundreds or thousands of years to change.

Just as a region's climate can change, Earth's climate can also change. These changes might be an increase or decrease in Earth's typical temperatures, how much rain or snow falls, or where rain and snow fall on the planet.

A certain amount of climate change is normal. Earth's climate is always changing. During its millions of years of history, there have been times when Earth's climate has been warmer or colder than it is now.

Earth's climate has changed when it received more or less sunlight, the sun's intensity varied, the atmosphere changed, or as the surface of the planet changed. Shifts in Earth's climate have generally lasted thousands to millions of years.

So, what's the big deal? If Earth's climate is always changing, why do we sound the alarm now on climate change?

Scientists who study Earth's climate have noticed that our planet is getting warmer much faster than in the past.

Earth's temperature has increased more than 1 degree Fahrenheit (more than half a degree Celsius) in only 100 years. This swift increase in Earth's surface temperature is called global warming. One degree might not seem like a big deal. But changes like this can have a big impact on Earth's climate and all of its inhabitants.

WHAT CAUSES CLIMATE CHANGE?

Many things can cause climate change. In the past, climate change occurred because of natural reasons that were not linked to human activity. Small changes in Earth's orbit can change the planet's distance from the sun. The sun can emit more or less energy. Oceans and landforms change. Volcanos erupt. All of these natural events can cause climate change.

Today, scientists believe Earth's current warming trend is not a natural event. Instead, they have found evidence that human activity is driving climate change. Let's look at how.

WHY CARBON DIOXIDE IS KEY

Carbon dioxide is one of several greenhouse gases in Earth's atmosphere. All greenhouse gases absorb and radiate heat. What makes carbon dioxide so important when talking about global warming and climate change? Carbon dioxide absorbs less heat per molecule than other greenhouse gases, including methane or nitrous oxide. However, carbon dioxide molecules are more plentiful in Earth's atmosphere. It also remains in the atmosphere much longer than methane or nitrous oxide. While less plentiful than water vapor, carbon dioxide absorbs some thermal energy that water vapor does not. Because of these characteristics, carbon dioxide is a critical factor in the atmosphere's greenhouse effect. Scientists estimate that increases in carbon dioxide in the atmosphere are significant drivers of Earth's temperature rise.

EARTH'S ATMOSPHERE

Earth's atmosphere is a layer of gases that surround the planet. This layer is made up mostly of nitrogen and oxygen gases. Other gases, such as argon, carbon dioxide, neon, helium, and hydrogen, are present, but in smaller amounts. The atmosphere is like a blanket that insulates and protects Earth. It absorbs the sun's heat and holds it inside the atmosphere to keep Earth warm. This process helps Earth's temperature to stay pretty steady. The atmosphere also protects Earth from the sun's radiation. There are five main layers in the atmosphere. Starting at Earth's surface and extending outward, the layers are the troposphere, stratosphere, mesosphere, thermosphere, and exosphere.

Since the Industrial Revolution, people have built factories to manufacture products. We drive cars and fly airplanes. We heat and cool homes, cook food, watch television, and use all sorts of electrical appliances. All of these activities need energy. Most of the time, we get the energy to power our cars and generate electricity by burning fossil fuels—coal, oil, and gas.

Burning fossil fuels releases greenhouse gases into the atmosphere. These gases can cause the atmosphere to warm.

GREENHOUSE GAS EFFECTS

Have you ever been inside a greenhouse that was being used to grow plants? What did it feel like? That heat and humidity happens because sunlight shines into the glass walls and roof of the greenhouse during the day. The walls and ceiling trap the heat inside, warming the air and plants. During cold nights or the winter season, the greenhouse stays warm.

Earth's atmosphere works like a greenhouse. Sunlight travels through the atmosphere and reaches Earth's surface. The surface absorbs the light and heat energy from that sunlight. At night, the surface cools and releases heat into the atmosphere. Gases in the atmosphere, including carbon dioxide, trap some of the heat near Earth's surface like a glass roof traps heat in the greenhouse.

Atmospheric gases that trap heat are called greenhouse gases. In Earth's atmosphere, greenhouse gases include water vapor, carbon dioxide, methane, nitrous oxide, and ozone.

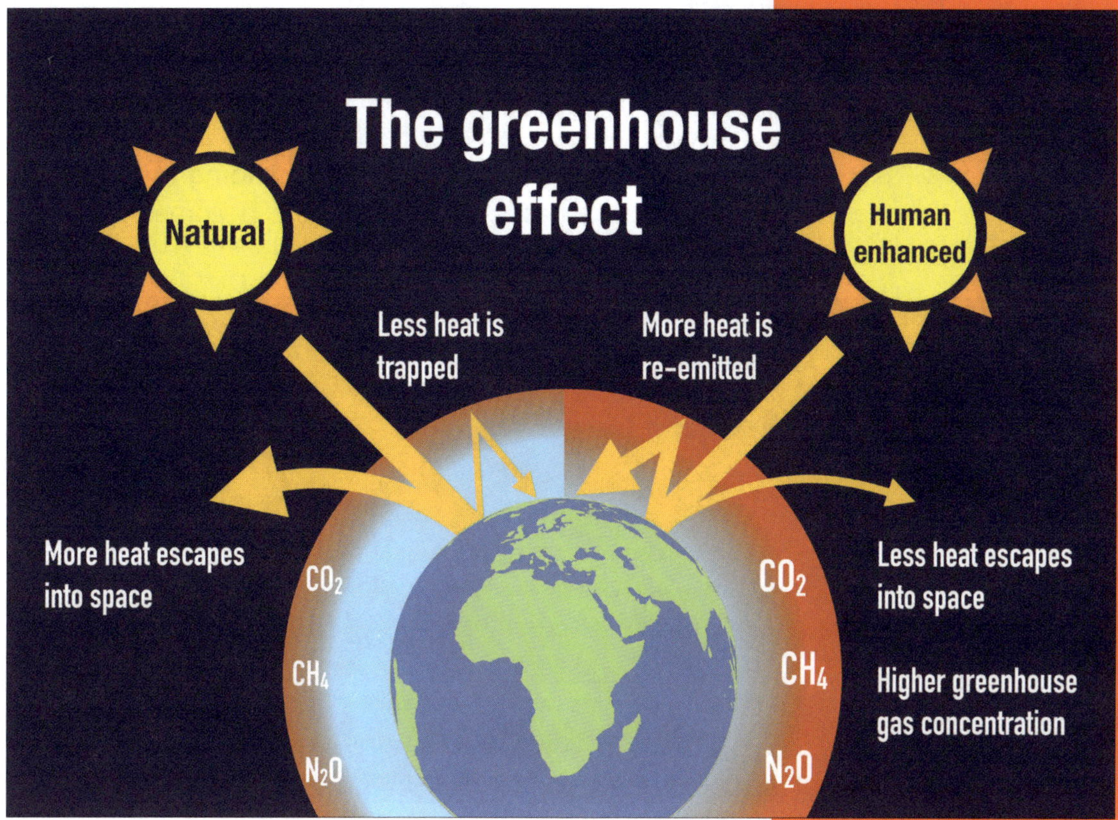

This process helps keep Earth at a livable temperature. If there were no greenhouse effect, Earth's surface would be an average of -0.4 degrees Fahrenheit (-18 degrees Celsius). Brrr!

As Earth's surface, waters, and air warm up, they emit heat energy. This energy is absorbed by water vapor and greenhouse gases in the atmosphere. In turn, the greenhouse gas and water molecules radiate heat in all directions. Some of that heat energy radiates back to Earth and further warms both the lower atmosphere and Earth's surface. It adds to the heat that the atmosphere and surface already absorb from direct sunlight. Greenhouse gases release the absorbed heat slowly through time, just like the bricks in a fireplace emit heat long after the fire is put out.

As more greenhouse gas molecules accumulate in Earth's atmosphere, more heat released from the surface is absorbed into the atmosphere. As that additional heat radiates back to Earth, the planet's surface temperature increases. By adding more greenhouse gases, the atmosphere becomes a hotter greenhouse.

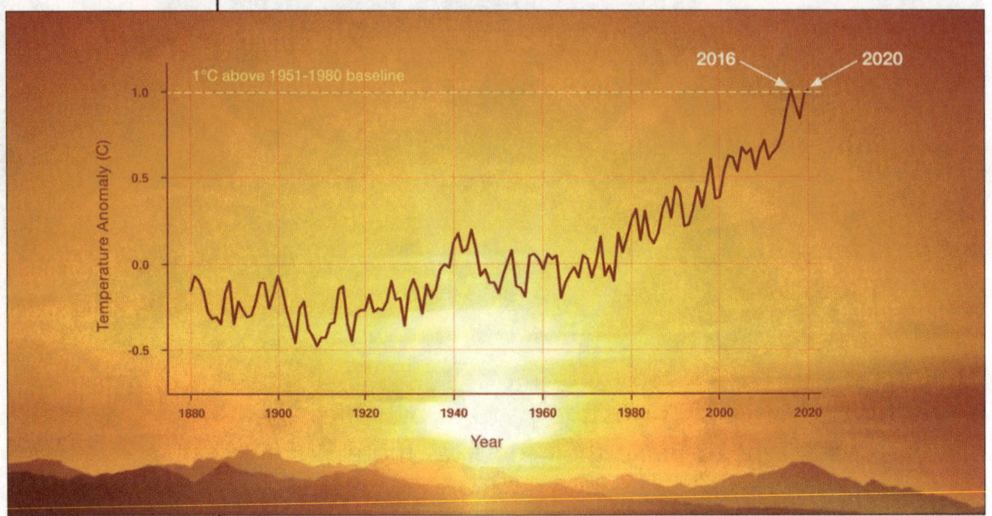

Credit: NASA/JPL-Caltech

WARMING FASTER THAN USUAL

Scientists who study the history of Earth's climate have found that the current rate of warming is much faster than previous warming events. The paleoclimate record shows that when Earth warmed after ice ages that happened during the last million years, global temperatures rose 7.2 to 12.6 degrees Fahrenheit (4 to 7 degrees Celsius) during the course of 5,000 years.

In the past 100 years, Earth's temperature has risen about 1.3 degrees Fahrenheit (0.7 degrees Celsius). This rise is about 10 times faster than past ice age warming rates.

CLIMATE CLUES

During one year, a mature tree absorbs more than 48 pounds of carbon dioxide from the atmosphere.

Scientific models predict that Earth will continue to warm between 3.6 and 10.8 degrees Fahrenheit (2 to 6 degrees Celsius) during the next century. That estimated rate of warming is about 20 times faster than previous warming periods, which is very unusual.

While Earth's climate has gone through warming periods before, scientists believe that natural causes alone cannot explain the rapid changes happening now. Instead, they point to human activities as the primary cause of Earth's current warming.

Since the Industrial Revolution, humans have been burning fossil fuels for energy at an increasing rate, releasing more greenhouse gases, including carbon dioxide, into the atmosphere. At the same time, humans have cleared forests to build houses, factories, roads, shopping malls, and more. Trees act as nature's air filters by absorbing carbon dioxide from the air to use in photosynthesis. This is the process by which plants use sunlight to make their food. As more forests are cleared, fewer trees are left to absorb the carbon dioxide in our atmosphere.

Scientists report that the annual rate of increase in carbon dioxide in the atmosphere in the last 60 years is 100 times faster than previous natural increases.

EVIDENCE OF PAST CLIMATES

Scientists learn about past climates by examining evidence found in nature. Tree rings, layers of glacier ice, layers of sedimentary rocks, ocean sediment, and coral reefs all hold clues about the climate on Earth thousands of years ago. For example, bubbles of air found in glacier ice contain tiny samples of Earth's atmosphere from years past. Analyzing these air bubbles can help scientists learn about the greenhouse gases in the atmosphere for the past 800,000 years. Also, the chemical makeup of the ice gives clues about the history of Earth's average temperatures. Using this evidence, scientists build paleoclimates, which are records of Earth's past climates. The paleoclimate record shows when past ice ages and periods of climate warming occurred.

VOCAB LAB 

Write down what you think each word means. What root words can you find to help you? What does the context of the word tell you?

atmosphere, **carbon dioxide**, **climate**, **climate change**, **fossil fuels**, **global warming**, **greenhouse gases**, **paleoclimate record**, and **weather**

Compare your definitions with those of your friends or classmates. Did you all come up with the same meanings? Turn to the text and glossary if you need help.

TEXT TO WORLD

Which of your activities use energy produced by fossil fuels?

WHY SHOULD WE CARE ABOUT CLIMATE CHANGE?

Scientists predict that Earth's current warming trend will continue at least for the next century. The impact of Earth's warming will be felt worldwide. As surface temperatures rise, more snow and ice will melt. Oceans will rise. Some regions will experience hotter temperatures, while other areas will have colder winters. Extreme weather events such as hurricanes, heatwaves, droughts, floods, and more will become common. Animals and plants will have to adapt to changes in their habitats or be forced to migrate. Certain diseases may become more common among humans.

CLIMATE CLUES

In 2019, carbon dioxide levels in the atmosphere were the highest in at least the past 800,000 years.

We are already seeing the effects of climate change around the world. Some areas have already begun to experience changing weather and more severe storms. Coastal communities are dealing with the impact of rising sea levels and flooding. Ecosystems are struggling with the loss of habitats and the migration of plant and animal species.

Climate change affects every living thing on Earth—including humans. This book explores the human impacts of climate change and how it affects people and communities every day. By learning about the science behind climate change and the real-life effects on our lives, you will be better prepared to navigate the new world and its changing climate.

KEY QUESTIONS

- **What symptoms of climate change have you noticed where you live?**
- **Do you think every person has a responsibility to do what they can to keep the planet healthy?**

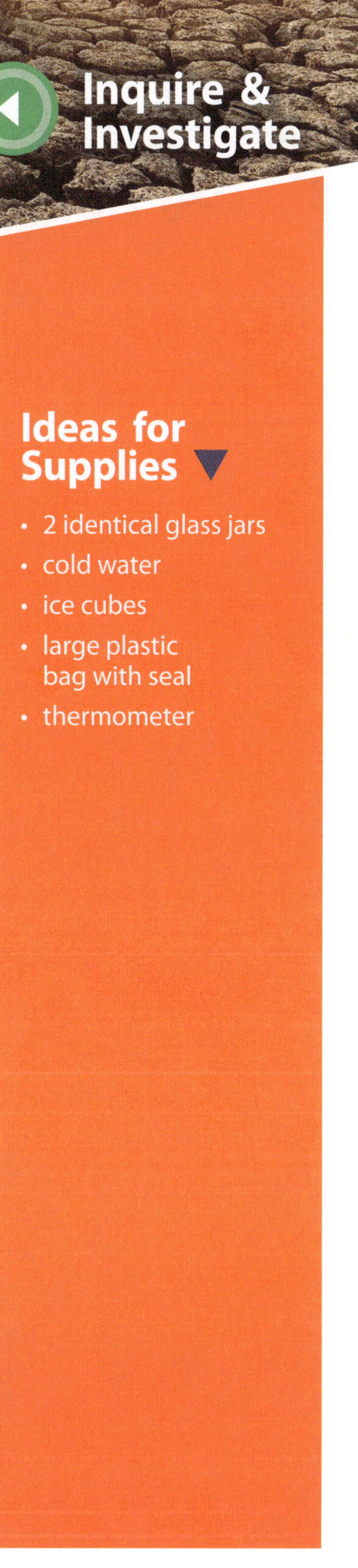

EXPLORE THE GREENHOUSE EFFECT

Sunlight warms the earth's atmosphere and surface. As the earth's surface, waters, and air get warmer, they release heat energy. Gases in the atmosphere absorb and radiate some of this heat back to Earth's surface. This process allows Earth to remain at a livable temperature. In this activity, we'll explore how the greenhouse effect works.

Ideas for Supplies

- 2 identical glass jars
- cold water
- ice cubes
- large plastic bag with seal
- thermometer

- **Create two identical environments.** Pour 2 cups of cold water and 4 ice cubes into each jar. Measure the temperature of the water in each jar. Record the data in your science notebook.
- **Place one of the jars in a sealed plastic bag.** Put both jars in a sunny spot. Make sure that both jars are receiving equal amounts of sunlight.
- **After an hour, measure the temperature of the water in each jar.** Record your results. How do the temperatures of the jars compare to each other? How do the temperatures compare to the earlier temperatures? How do your results demonstrate the greenhouse effect? How does what you learned relate to global warming and climate change?

To investigate more, repeat this activity with more jars and different types of coverings. Try putting jars in colored plastic bags, cloth bags, or paper bags. Try punching holes in the plastic bag. What if you repeat the activity in a non-sunny area? How do these changes impact your results?

Chapter 1

Severe Storms and Extreme Weather

What is the link between climate change and extreme weather?

As the atmosphere and the oceans heat up, droughts, wildfires, floods, and storms all become a more frequent part of our lives.

In July 2021, the tiny town of Lytton in British Columbia, Canada, set a record few people wanted. In the midst of an extraordinary heat wave, Lytton hit 121.3 degrees Fahrenheit (49.6 degrees Celsius), the highest temperature ever recorded in Canada. Usually, temperatures in this mountain town hover around 77 degrees Fahrenheit (25 degrees Celsius) in June. But in 2021, it was almost 50 degrees hotter! The overnight temperatures were hotter than the town's usual daytime temperatures.

Meghan Fandrich, who lives in Lytton, said it was "almost impossible" to spend time outside in the heat. Like many people in the area, she does not have air conditioning at home.

To keep the house cool, she tried to keep the door shut. She also spent as much time as possible at the air-conditioned coffee shop that she owns. She sent her five-year-old daughter to stay with family in Mission, British Columbia, where temperatures were a bit cooler.

That same dangerous heat wave stretched across western Canada and the Pacific Northwest region of the United States. The unbearable heat closed schools and businesses. In Portland, Oregon, the light-rail and streetcar system halted as the extreme heat melted cables. In Washington state, the pavement buckled in the heat. And in Vancouver, Canada, it was so hot that some people fried eggs on their terraces. Wildfires burned in the hot, dry environment and crops wilted in the fields.

Paramedics and emergency room staff treated hundreds of people with heat-related illnesses.

Dozens died from heat-related causes, such as heatstroke. Eighty-five-year-old Dorothy G. from Seattle, Washington, was one of the heat's victims. According to the medical examiner, the older woman died of hyperthermia—her body overheated. She lived alone in a home without air conditioning. News of her passing from the heat stunned her neighbors.

Read more stories about Canada's heat wave in this article.

What are some ways you can stay safe when the temperature rises to uncomfortable degrees?

Canada heat wave

BECOME A CLIMATOLOGIST

A climatologist is an atmospheric scientist who studies Earth's climate. Climatologists collect and analyze climate data from soil, water, air, ice cores, plant life, and more. They search for patterns in weather and analyze how weather patterns affect Earth and everything that lives on the planet. Sometimes, climatologists study climates from years past. These scientists work both in the field collecting samples and information and also in a lab or office. The research they conduct can be used for various purposes, including building design, weather forecasting, agricultural planning, and more.

Although it is impossible to link the historic heat wave to climate change directly, many scientists strongly believe it is related. "Climate change is increasing the frequency, intensity, and duration of heat waves," said Kristie Ebi, a professor at the University of Washington Center for Health and the Global Environment. "When you look at this heat wave, it is so far outside the range of normal."

THE FIRST SIGNS: EXTREME WEATHER

Extreme weather is one of the earliest signs of climate change. But what makes weather extreme? Weather becomes extreme when it is very different from what is normal weather for a place at a particular time of year.

Have you ever heard of a 100-year storm? Extreme weather is often described by how often it occurs—every decade, century, or longer. Extreme weather often lasts many days or months and can affect many people.

CLIMATE CLUES

Heat waves kill more people in the United States than all other weather-related natural disasters combined.

Some extreme weather is normal. However, climate change is affecting the frequency and intensity of extreme weather events.

For example, hurricanes are common in some areas. But climate change can make every stage of a hurricane more intense and damaging. Similarly, climate change can make other extreme weather events—droughts, wildfires, floods, and storms—more frequent and severe.

EXTREME HEAT: GETTING HOTTER

Around the world, hot days are becoming hotter and more frequent. That doesn't mean cold regions have no cold days. Instead, it means that global warming is causing more intensely hot days and fewer of those cold days.

This trend of hotter temperatures is already occurring across the United States. According to the U.S. Environmental Protection Agency (EPA), sweltering summer days have become more common during the past few decades. And it's not just the days! Scorching summer nights have increased at an even faster rate. At the same time, extremely cold winter days are becoming less common.

Credit: Holly Salzman (CC BY 2.0)

Heat waves are also becoming more frequent. A heat wave is unusually hot weather that lasts for two or more days.

During a heat wave, the temperatures exceed the average temperatures for the area. What might be a heat wave in one place, however, might be normal weather in another place. For example, several days of greater than 95-degree weather in Maine are unusual, but those same temperatures are normal on summer days in Arizona.

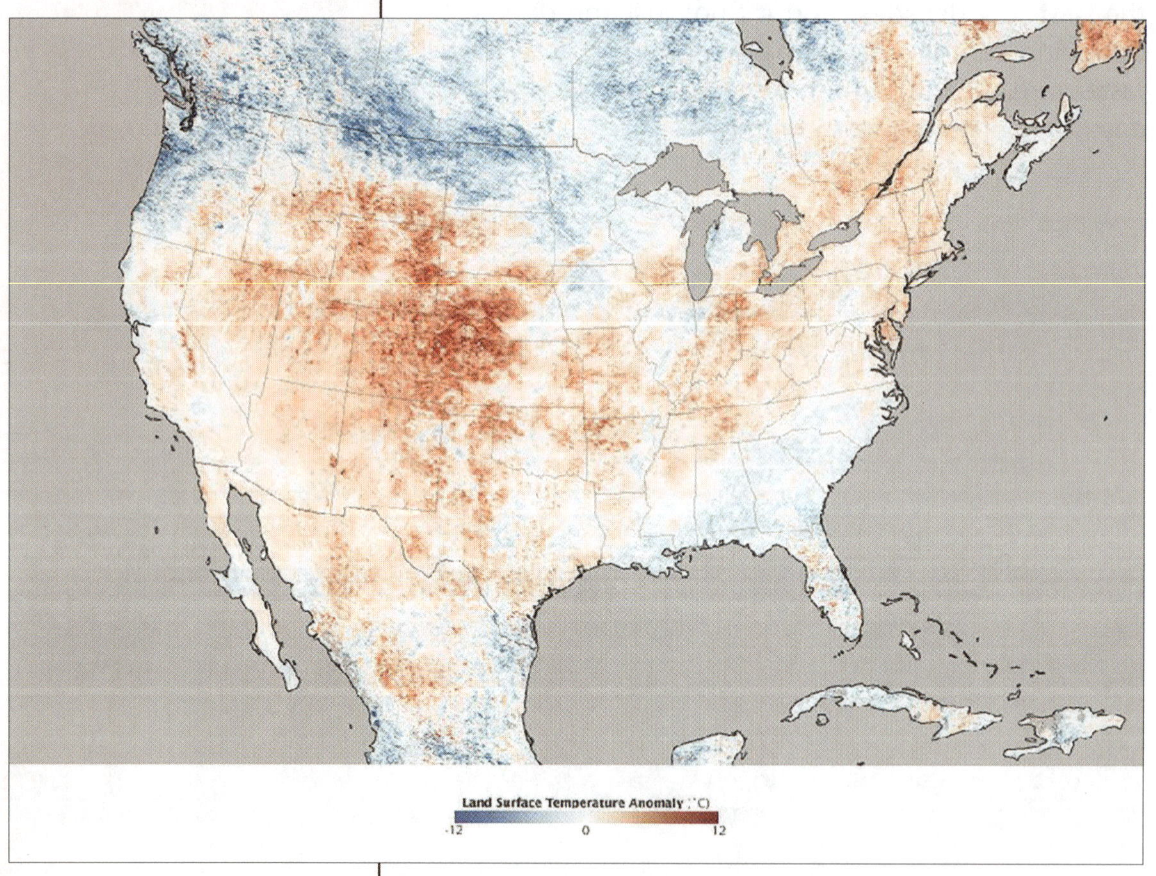

A map of land surface temperature June 17–24, 2012, during a heat wave

Credit: NASA Earth Observatory image by Jesse Allen

Heat waves form from trapped air. Usually, Earth's atmosphere moves cool, dry air (high-pressure systems) and warm, moist air (low-pressure systems) along Earth's surface.

Sometimes, a high-pressure system stops moving and settles over an area. The downward push of sinking cooler air prevents warmer air near the ground from rising. The stalled high-pressure system acts as a cap, or heat dome, that traps warm air and heat near Earth's surface. The lack of rising air also prevents rain from forming and cooling the hot air. As a result, heat builds at the surface and a heat wave forms.

In 2012, parts of North America experienced one of the most intense heat waves in history. A high-pressure system moved north from Mexico and grew. At the end of June, the system hovered over the U.S. Great Plains. It spread east and north and settled over the center of North America through July 2012. It acted like an oven, trapping air and warming it.

Heat waves can be dangerous. In 2012, more than 80 people died of heat-related causes during the North American heat wave. Many more became ill.

Record-setting temperatures and heat waves are a normal part of weather. However, as Earth's climate warms, scientists predict heat waves will become more common and more severe.

HIGHS AND LOWS

Have you ever heard a meteorologist talk about high-pressure systems and low-pressure systems? A high-pressure system is a swirling mass of cool, dry air. Its winds spiral out from a high-pressure center. High-pressure systems usually bring sunny, fair weather and light winds. A low-pressure system is a mass of warm, moist air. Its strong winds spiral in toward a low-pressure center. Low-pressure systems generally bring stormy weather and strong winds.

DRYING UP THE LAND

How many ways do you use water every day? We drink water and use it to grow the food we eat. We use water to wash clothes, cook, shower, and swim. Some electrical power plants even use water to produce the electricity needed to watch television, turn on lights, play video games, and more.

Check out this United Nations interactive model that shows how climate change will shape weather worldwide.

What do the models tell you about the climate in your region in 50 years? One hundred years?

IPCC interactive

Sometimes, there is a shortage in the water supply. This often happens when a region experiences less precipitation—rain or snow—than usual. With less precipitation, there is less moisture in soil and less surface water and groundwater. A drought is a period of abnormally low precipitation that leads to a water shortage. It can last for weeks, months, or years. In some areas, drought conditions can last for a decade! The longer a drought lasts, the more harm it does.

When a drought hits an area, it can reduce the community's water supplies.

If normal water supplies cannot provide enough clean drinking water, communities must bring in drinking water from other places, which can be very expensive. Plus, crops need water to grow. Without enough precipitation to water crops naturally, farmers must use irrigation. But, in a drought, farmers might not be able to bring in enough water from local rivers or streams to irrigate their crops. The crops may wilt and die.

Climate change can make droughts more frequent, longer, and wider spread. In warmer temperatures, water evaporates more quickly. Combined with less than usual precipitation, the soil becomes more parched than usual. Lakes, rivers, streams, and other water sources dry out.

BURNING LONGER AND FARTHER

In the United States, people cause more than 80 percent of wildfires. A fire begins after someone drops a lit cigarette or fails to put out a campfire. Lightning strikes spark a smaller number of wildfires. While climate change does not start wildfires, it can make them more extreme. Once a fire starts, hot, dry conditions make it easier for the fire to spread quickly and more challenging to put out.

Changes in Earth's climate are making some areas on the planet hotter and drier. Here's how. Greenhouse gases cause global temperatures to rise. Warmer temperatures increase water evaporation, and the atmosphere draws more moisture from the soil, which makes the land drier. Warmer temperatures also mean earlier snowmelt, which causes soil to be dry for longer periods. These dry soils are more vulnerable to fire.

Even a slight increase in temperatures can have a severe effect on wildfires. Scientists project that an average annual temperature increase of 1.8 degrees Fahrenheit (1 degree Celsius) in the western United States would increase the amount of land burned by wildfires each year by as much as 600 percent in some forests.

CLIMATE CLUES

Studies show that the large forest fires of recent years are burning more than six times the land area and lasting nearly five times longer than in earlier decades.

MOISTURE STRESS AND PLANTS

Under normal conditions, plants release water vapor into the air from tiny openings called stomata on leaves, stems, and flowers. This process is called transpiration. If there is little precipitation and the soil is dry, plants experience moisture stress and they release less water vapor into the air. Less water vapor in the atmosphere reduces precipitation, further drying the soil and putting more moisture stress on the plant.

Wildfires damage property and infrastructure. They also threaten human, animal, and plant life. When fires burn entire forests, they destroy essential habitats for plants and animals. Extreme fires can even make greenhouse gas emissions worse. Trees absorb and store carbon dioxide from the atmosphere. The more trees are destroyed by fire, the less carbon they can absorb from the atmosphere. This contributes to global warming and eventually causes more fires.

CLIMATE CLUES

California firefighters are using computer modeling to assess fire risk and predict a fire's path and growth. This information allows them to position equipment and crews to respond more quickly.

In June 2017, an extreme wildfire raged uncontrollably through parts of central Portugal. Thousands of firefighters battled the flames as the fire spread across tens of thousands of acres of land. By the time firefighters got the fire under control, 66 people had been killed and more than 250 others were injured. The fire also destroyed nearly 500 houses. Many of the fire's victims were trapped in their homes or cars as they tried to escape.

Lidia Antunes and her family were some of the lucky ones. When the fire broke out, Antunes's family fled their home in three cars. As they raced down flaming forest roads, the cars quickly lost each other. "I was convinced I was going to die. I was speeding through flames and it was so hot, I thought if I tried to U-turn the car would melt," Antunes said. "At some point I got lost and got hit by another car but I just kept speeding. I knew that as soon as the car stopped I would die."

CLIMATE CLUES

Forest fires act as nature's way to clear out undergrowth on the forest floor, clearing space for larger, mature trees to grow. However, the increase in extreme and uncontrollable wildfires is destroying entire forests.

As she drove, Antunes came upon a couple pleading for help. "I told them to get in quickly, but the back doors of the car had melted, so the two of them had to get in through the passenger's window. An older man who was with them couldn't get in and decided to stay behind. To this day, I have no idea if he survived," she said.

HEAVIER PRECIPITATION

Earth's rising temperatures can also make wet regions wetter. Warmer air increases water evaporation and draws more moisture from Earth's soil, lakes, rivers, and other water sources. Because of this, the amount of water vapor in the atmosphere increases. When weather conditions are right, storms turn the increased water vapor in the atmosphere into heavier rain or snow.

In this way, climate change makes certain regions wetter.

Read more about the wildfire in Portugal that terrified Antunes and her family.

BBC Portugal wildfire

PESTS AND WILDFIRES

Did you know that tiny pests can make wildfires worse? An outbreak of destructive insects can kill large numbers of trees in a forest. Dead, dry trees are an ideal fuel for burning fires. Increases in pest outbreaks in some areas can be traced back to climate change. As temperatures warm, some insects take advantage of the longer summer mating season to breed more and reproduce faster. This has led to pest outbreaks the size of which haven't been seen for hundreds of years.

The warming of Arctic regions may be disrupting the polar vortex, strong winds that enclose a pool of extremely cold air near the North Pole. If the polar vortex is disrupted, cold, icy air can move farther south and trigger winter storms in places where they are uncommon.

While some areas are getting drier, others are getting wetter. In the United States, many people already experience heavier precipitation. In the continental United States, rainfall in 2018 broke historical records. An average of 36.2 inches fell during the year, 6 inches more than the average yearly rainfall. According to the EPA, since 1901, total annual precipitation has increased in the United States at a rate of 0.20 inches per decade.

Heavier rain or snow means more than umbrellas or snow shovels. Even a small change in precipitation can have many impacts on humans and ecosystems.

Flooding in the Netherlands in July 2021

The amount of rainfall affects groundwater and surface water used for drinking, irrigating crops, and other uses. Changes in precipitation impact the animals and plants that live in an area and affect the health of rivers, lakes, and streams.

CLIMATE CLUES

Scientists predict that slow-moving storms that bring heavy rainfall like those that flooded parts of Europe will become more common by the year 2100 because of climate change.

In some cases, extreme precipitation causes severe flooding. In July 2021, major floods swept across Germany, Belgium, and other parts of Central Europe. The flooding was caused by a low-pressure weather system that moved slowly and stalled over Europe.

In the hardest-hit areas of Germany, two months' worth of rain fell in 24 hours! Many places recorded more than 6 inches of rain during a two- to three-day period. Some areas recorded even more. For example, the Reifferscheid region in Germany recorded more than 8 inches of rain in nine hours.

These massive amounts of rain caused rivers and sewage systems to overflow. Flash floods trapped people in their homes. Many people climbed on their roofs and waited for rescue. Floodwaters poured down streets like rivers, swept away cars, and destroyed houses and buildings. Hundreds of thousands of people lost power, communications, and water supplies.

More than 200 people died. Thousands of police, soldiers, and emergency workers worked furiously to save people.

HOW DOES CLIMATE CHANGE CAUSE FLOODING?

As Earth's temperature rises, it causes more water to evaporate and become water vapor in the atmosphere. More water vapor in the atmosphere means larger amounts of rain or snow. When an intense rain falls all at once, it overwhelms Earth's surface. Rivers, streams, and lakes overflow. Soil cannot absorb so much water in so little time. The excess water has nowhere to go and turns into a flood.

FLOODING DISASTER IN TENNESSEE

In 2021, record-breaking rain in central Tennessee triggered deadly flash flooding. One observation site reported 17 inches of rain in only 24 hours, an amount much higher than the state record rainfall of almost 14 inches in 1982. The extreme rainfall caused catastrophic flooding. In the small town of Waverly, floodwaters swept through town and trapped residents on their rooftops and in vehicles. The flooding damaged homes and property and flipped cars. At least 21 people died, with dozens still missing a few days after the floods. Many believe climate change played a role in the extreme weather that devastated the area.

In some areas, the flooding destroyed entire villages. Gregor Jericho lives in Rheinbach, a town in Germany. He described the devastation of his hometown and said, "It's a very sad scene. Streets, bridges, and some buildings are destroyed. There's garbage everywhere. Parts of buildings are in the road, people are sitting and crying. It's so sad. People have lost their homes, their cars are in fields flooded. My city looks like a battle has taken place."

Another Rheinbach resident, Ansgar Rehbein, described the moment the floods hit. "Once the river started overflowing and the water came down from the hillside, it was a matter of two minutes before the courtyard was flooded with waist-high water. We had to get out through the window and uphill in order to save ourselves."

DESTRUCTIVE HURRICANES AND SUMMER STORMS

Hurricanes are some of the most powerful and destructive storms on Earth. A hurricane forms when warm, moist air near the ocean surface rises. This rising air creates a low-pressure area near the ocean surface. As the warm air rises, cooler air from nearby areas with higher air pressure pushes into the low-pressure area and replaces it. As the warm, moist air rises, it cools. The water vapor in the air forms clouds. The group of clouds spins and grows, fed by the ocean's heat and evaporating water vapor. As this process repeats itself, a hurricane can form.

Hurricanes need warm water to form—an ocean temperature of at least 80 degrees Fahrenheit at the surface. That's why you never hear of hurricanes in the Arctic Ocean!

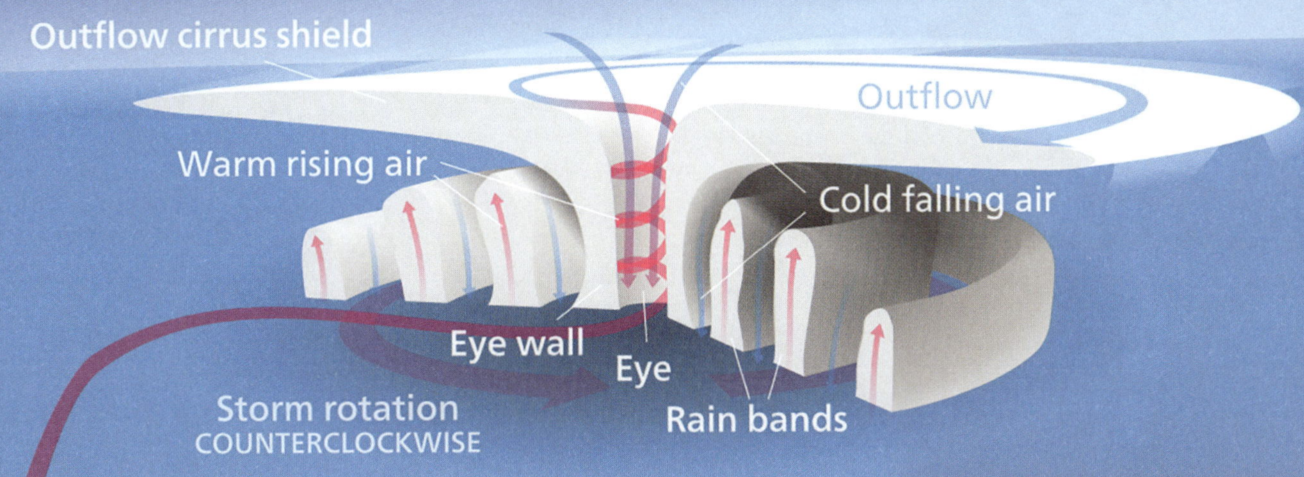

This diagram shows the different parts of a hurricane.

Credit: Kelvinsong (CC BY 2.0)

When hurricanes make landfall, they can create significant damage. These storms bring high winds, heavy rains, storm surges, and even tornadoes.

Scientists believe that Earth's warming climate makes hurricanes more powerful and more destructive. Warmer ocean surface temperatures provide more fuel to hurricanes. They become wetter and drop more precipitation in their path. For example, in 2017, Hurricane Harvey dropped more than 60 inches of rain over Texas, an extreme event that triggered dangerous flooding.

The warming climate also increases the speed of tropical storm winds, which can cause more damage to coastal regions. As tropical storms and hurricanes become wider-reaching, more frequent, and more intense, more communities will be at risk.

Read more about the 2021 flooding in Central Europe in this article.

What are some ways you can stay safe during a flood?

Europe flood 2021

A view of Hurricane Florence from space in 2018

Credit: NASA

Extreme heat waves, drought, rainfall, flooding, winter storms, hurricanes, and other weather events have impacted millions worldwide. How you experience extreme weather may be different from a friend on the other side of the world. While some people are dealing with rain and flooding, others struggle with drought and wildfires.

Despite these differences, extreme weather puts many people and communities at risk. It's one of the more visible signs of climate change.

CLIMATE CLUES

Hurricanes are called hurricanes only in the North Atlantic region. In the western Pacific, the same storms are known as typhoons, while between Australia and Africa, they are called cyclones.

MAKE CHANGE

As extreme weather becomes more common worldwide, people will learn to live and adapt to the weather events in their communities.

To reduce some of the worst impacts of extreme weather, families can make an emergency plan. You'll first need to understand what type of extreme weather is most likely to hit your area. Then, gather necessary water, food, batteries, and medication for an emergency kit. Decide how you will contact each other if separated and pick a family meeting place that is easy to find. Monitor weather forecasts and news alerts when the weather is expected. And make a plan to evacuate an area when weather makes it too dangerous to stay.

People can also take small steps at home to fight climate change and extreme weather.

Most people can find ways to reduce their energy use and pollution in their daily lives. For example, planting shade trees and shutting window shades can reduce air conditioning and energy needs. Walking, riding a bike, or carpooling reduces gasoline use and air pollution. These steps and more can reduce the amount of greenhouse gases released into the air, which can help combat global warming and the extreme weather it causes.

KEY QUESTIONS

- **How is extreme weather related to climate change?**
- **What are some precautions you can take to better survive extreme weather events?**

VOCAB LAB 

Write down what you think each word means. What root words can you find to help you? What does the context of the word tell you?

groundwater, **heat wave**, **heatstroke**, **high-pressure system**, **infrastructure**, **irrigation**, **low-pressure system**, **precipitation**, and **tropical storm**

Compare your definitions with those of your friends or classmates. Did you all come up with the same meanings? Turn to the text and glossary if you need help.

TEXT TO WORLD

How can you help your community prepare for extreme weather?

Inquire & Investigate

EXPLORE THE CHANGING CLIMATE IN YOUR TOWN

Climate change takes place during long periods, such as years, decades, centuries, or more. Climate change affects everyone differently. How has climate change affected the climate in your town? In this activity, we'll use the internet to investigate how climate has changed where you live through time.

- **To start, search the internet for historical temperature data for your local area.** If you cannot find data for your town, choose another town that has available data. Some websites that have historical weather data include:

Weather Underground

National Weather Service

Climate Data Online

The Old Farmer's Almanac

- **Once you have picked a location, how far back does the historical data go?** Choose a series of months and years to look up the historical average temperature recorded. For example, you might look up the monthly temperature averages in 1940, 1980, and 2020.

Inquire & Investigate

- **Create a data table to record and organize the data.** It might look something like this.

Average Monthly Temperatures

	1940	1980	2020
Jan			
Feb			
Mar			
Apr			
May			
June			
July			
Aug			
Sept			
Oct			
Nov			
Dec			

- **After you've collected all of the data, make a separate graph of each year's data.** Plot each month's average temperature on the graph. Repeat for each year on your chart. What do you notice from the charts?
- **To compare the years, create a single chart that plots each year's data in a different color.** How has the average temperature in your town changed through the years? Has it increased, decreased, or stayed the same? Do you notice any patterns in your data or recurring cycles? Were there any significant weather events during the years you chose that would affect the monthly temperature averages? How does the data show what is happening to climate in your town?

To investigate more, choose another town in a different part of the country that experiences different weather and climate from your town. Collect data from both locations on the same dates. Compare the two local climates. What differences and similarities do you notice? How has climate change affected the faraway town? Compare that to how climate change has affected your town.

Inquire & Investigate

HOT AIR RISING

During the summer, does it feel hotter on a higher floor in a building than on a lower floor? When air heats up, its molecules expand and spread out. The hot air becomes less dense and rises through denser, cooler air. As the warm air molecules rise through the cool air, they cool down, move closer together, become denser, and start to sink again. This movement of air rising and falling results in currents.

Usually, Earth's atmosphere moves cool, dry air (high-pressure systems) and warm, moist air (low-pressure systems) along Earth's surface. Sometimes, a high-pressure system stops moving and settles over an area, forcing air downward and trapping hot air near Earth's surface. As a result, heat builds up at the surface. A heat wave forms.

In this activity, we'll use water to demonstrate how hot air rises and cool air falls in the atmosphere.

Ideas for Supplies

- small glass jar
- water
- food coloring
- plastic wrap
- rubber band
- large glass jar (big enough to hold small jar)
- knife

- **Fill the small jar with very hot water.** Add several drops of food coloring to the hot water.
- **Stretch plastic wrap over the top of the jar.** Use a rubber band to secure and seal the plastic wrap to the jar top. Does the plastic wrap rise a little? Why do you think this happens?
- **Fill the large jar with cold water.** Gently place the small jar inside the large one. Use tongs if the small jar is too hot to hold.
- **Carefully use the knife to cut an opening in the plastic wrap on the small jar.** What happens? Does the colored water rise or fall? Does it stay in the jar? How does what you observed in this activity demonstrate the rise and fall of air currents in the atmosphere?

To investigate more, repeat this activity but do not slice the plastic wrap on the small jar. What happens to the colored water? How does this model show what happens during a heat wave?

Chapter 2

Food and Water Scarcity

How does climate change affect our food supply?

From temperature to moisture levels to contaminants, climate is directly linked to the quantity and quality of the meat, fruits, and vegetables we rely on to live.

The Bullen family farm on 4,000 acres outside Pilliga, Australia, grows wheat and barley and raises sheep. In recent years, the land has been too dry to plant. Their herd of sheep has dropped significantly, from 1,700 to 500 animals. Many farmers and ranchers across Australia are experiencing the same drop in their herds of sheep and cattle. In Queensland, farmer Kent Morris has seen his sheep numbers drop from 3,000 to 700 animals and his cattle drop from 300 to 12 animals.

Why? Since 2012, Australia has been in its hottest drought in history. The hot, dry conditions have devastated the continent's cattle ranches, sheep farms, and farm crops. The lack of water has been so severe that several of Morris's ewes stopped moving one day and laid under a tree to die. Morris says that it is impossible to plan for a drought this severe.

"I've kind of given up on cleaning," said Krystal Bullen in 2019, about the dust that coated her windows and home. "We've had droughts before, but nothing of this caliber."

For the remaining animals on the farm, the drought has dried up the grass they graze. Farmers must import feed from other places to feed their animals, which is expensive and time-consuming.

The drought conditions have also weakened the sheep and cattle. When they wander into dried-up creeks, the animals often become stuck in the mud. Predators such as giant monitor lizards eat the trapped animals. Farmers are forced to spend more time protecting their animals.

Read more about Australia's drought in this article.

How does drought affect the world food supply?

Caution: This article includes a photo some will find disturbing.

Time Australia drought

An Australian farmer worries about his sheep during a drought.

HEAT-TOLERANT WHEAT CROPS

As Earth continues to warm, many areas where wheat crops grow will experience rising temperatures. To help wheat crops thrive in a warmer world, scientists are working to identify genetic and molecular factors that affect wheat's ability to tolerate heat. Researchers are also using software models and real-time field observations to understand better how heat waves affect wheat. Plant breeders are studying wheat crops that thrive in hotter climates, such as India, Mexico, and Pakistan, and introducing these plants into their breeding programs. With all of this information, they hope to develop wheat crop lines with a high-temperature tolerance and a stable yield.

Climate scientists believe the intensity of Australia's drought is linked to climate change. Like many places around the world, Australia has been slowly getting warmer. Since 2005, the country has experienced nine of the 10 warmest years on record.

The struggles in Australia highlight how warming temperatures threaten the world's food and water supplies.

DECREASING FOOD SUPPLIES

In 2020, 7.8 billion people lived on Earth. The world's population is projected to grow to almost 10 billion by 2050. Every single person depends on food and water to survive. Yet scientists warn that climate change and its impacts—including higher temperatures, more extreme weather, droughts, increasing amounts of carbon dioxide in the atmosphere, and rising sea levels—are threats to the world's food supplies.

People worldwide rely on crops grown in the United States and other countries for their food supplies. Rising temperatures threaten these crops in several ways. For example, warmer temperatures affect crop yield—how much of a crop can be grown and harvested on a piece of land. Most crops have an ideal temperature at which they grow best. If temperatures are higher, the crop will not grow as well. Heat stress can disrupt the plant's natural life cycle processes, including pollination, flowering, root development, and growth. When this happens, crop yields decline. The farm produces less food.

Corn is an example of this problem. As the world's most produced and traded crop, corn is an essential part of our food supply.

Corn is also used to feed livestock and make biofuels. In a 2018 study, researchers found that warming temperatures have a significant negative effect on how corn grows. Climate scientists currently predict that Earth will warm between 3.6 and 10.8 degrees Fahrenheit (2 to 6 degrees Celsius) by 2100 if nothing is done to limit greenhouse gas emissions. This temperature increase could cause corn production to drop by almost half in the United States.

Even if temperatures warmed by only 3.6 degrees Fahrenheit (2 degrees Celsius), scientists predict corn production would drop by 18 percent.

It's not just corn in the United States that is at risk. The researchers found that the world's top-producing corn regions—Brazil, Argentina, and Ukraine—would all suffer significant drops in corn yield as temperatures rise. If the corn supply drops worldwide, it could affect the food supply for everyone and drive up the price of corn.

Read more about sustainable agriculture in this article.

How do sustainable agriculture practices impact climate change?

UCS sustainable agriculture

RICE AT RISK

Climate scientists predict that drought and water shortages will become more common in many places around the world. They expect water shortages to affect the production of rice, a staple food for more than half the people living on Earth. During severe droughts, rainfed rice production has dropped 17 to 40 percent. More than 57 million acres of rainfed rice in areas of South and Southeast Asia are already experiencing water shortages. In Africa, recurring drought affects nearly 80 percent of rainfed rice-growing regions. Do you eat rice at your house? How might your family's grocery bill be affected if less rice is produced, and it becomes more expensive?

Warming temperatures also affect vegetables, fruits, and legumes. In another 2018 study, researchers found that vegetables and legumes can be even more vulnerable to rising temperatures and heat stress than grains such as corn.

Researchers predict that if global warming continues at its current pace, vegetable and legume crops may drop by 35 percent by 2100.

EXTREME WEATHER AND PESTS

What do crops need to grow besides ideal temperature? Water! Farmers depend on predictable rainfall to water their crops. In some areas, climate change is changing rainfall patterns. Some regions are struggling with too little rainfall and drought. Without enough water, many crops wither and die.

CLIMATE CLUES

American farmers provide nearly 25 percent of all grains (wheat, corn, and rice) to the world.

Other places are dealing with too much rain. As we learned in the last chapter, when temperatures rise, more water evaporates into the atmosphere. Warmer air holds more moisture, which can make rainstorms more intense. Extreme precipitation can damage crops and can also trigger flooding that drowns crops. Flooding often carries sewage and pollutants from roads, farms, and lawns into fields of crops and eventually our food.

A flooded farm in Nova Scotia, Canada

Extreme weather can destroy entire farms or prevent crops from growing. Farmer Dale Murden has grown citrus in southern Texas since the 1980s. In the past few years, Murden's farm has been battered by a series of extreme weather events.

In 2020, Murden's citrus trees struggled to survive during a massive drought. The hot, dry weather withered the trees' leaves and fruits. Next, a hurricane hit the region. The storm's destructive rains and winds hurled thousands of unripe grapefruits to the ground, ruining them all. Then, in February 2021, a freak deep freeze hit Texas. Frost split branches on the citrus trees, browned leaves, and sent more fruit to the ground. The deep freeze cost at least $600 million in lost crops and livestock across Texas.

"I've been doing this for over 40 years, and I've lived through hurricanes, freezes, and droughts," Murden said, "but never in my life have I experienced all three in one year."

UPSIDES

Sometimes, changes in a region's temperature are beneficial to a crop. For example, a temperature increase up to two degrees would increase the production of corn, wheat, and grass crops in Denmark. In some cases, warming temperatures may bring the average temperatures in an area closer to a crop's ideal growing temperature. When this happens, the higher temperatures improve the crop's growing conditions and crop yields increase. Warming temperatures may also allow farmers to plant new crops that could previously grow only in warmer regions.

Learn more about extreme weather events in Texas in this article.

Can you think of ways to protect crops from extreme weather?

extreme weather Texas

As extreme weather becomes more common worldwide, more farms and ranches will be battered like Murden's citrus trees. Heavy rains prevent farmers from planting crops. Wildfires destroy thousands of acres, while hurricanes disrupt farming operations. Billions of dollars of damage threaten the food supply and the ability of farms to produce the food we eat.

Warming temperatures, earlier springs, and milder winters may also allow weeds, pests, and fungi to attack and damage crops. Pests and weeds are usually killed by cold weather, but warmer temperatures let them stick around longer, putting more crops at risk. Sometimes, warmer temperatures allow pests and plant diseases to move into new areas that used to be too cold for them to survive.

Wheat rust on oats in Algeria

Credit: Abdelmoumen Taoutaou

Faced with new types of disease and pests for the first time, crops have few defenses against them. For example, a fungal infection called wheat rust recently surfaced in Africa.

Wheat rust had not been seen in that region for more than 50 years. Warmer temperatures allowed the disease to attack crops and spread to Asia, the Middle East, and Europe.

DECLINING NUTRITION

In addition to the rising heat, increasing amounts of carbon dioxide in the atmosphere can affect crops. Under perfect conditions, higher carbon dioxide levels can increase plant growth. However, the additional growth comes with a cost: nutrition.

Researchers have found that when carbon dioxide increases, a plant's protein content may drop. In one study, researchers found that if carbon dioxide levels continue to climb, crops such as barley, wheat, potatoes, and rice will have 6 to 15 percent lower protein content.

The concentrations of important minerals and vitamins in plants are also projected to drop as carbon dioxide levels climb. When carbon dioxide in the atmosphere increases, the tiny openings in plant leaves shrink and they lose less water. As plants lose less water, their circulation slows. They draw in fewer minerals from the soil and produce fewer vitamins.

For example, rice grown in conditions with high carbon dioxide had between 13 and 30 percent less of the various vitamin Bs than rice grown at normal carbon dioxide levels.

As the nutrients in our food decline, more people will be at risk of malnutrition. Livestock that feed on lower-nutrient crops will also be in danger.

DISRUPTING FOOD DISTRIBUTION

Extreme weather such as heavy storms, floods, and drought can disrupt food distribution. If transportation is delayed or diverted, it may not reach food producers. And if food is not stored correctly, it can spoil and become contaminated. When people or animals eat spoiled food, they often get sick.

Read about Australian inventor Saul Griffith, who wants to stop global warming by decarbonizing every American household.

What changes could you make in your home?

Saul Griffith climate solutions

LIVESTOCK IN TROUBLE

Climate change affects more than plants and crops. It also affects animals directly and indirectly, which can impact the world's food supply. We rely on livestock for food such as meat, eggs, and milk.

CLIMATE CLUES

Many livestock graze on wild plants and grasses. A drought means less quality vegetation to graze upon, and the animals may produce less food and become more vulnerable to disease.

Extreme heat causes heat stress in livestock and can eventually make livestock less fertile and less able to reproduce. It can also make livestock more vulnerable to disease. In dairy cows, heat stress can reduce milk production.

In some regions, drought is forcing ranchers to reduce the size of their herds. The average adult cow weighs about 1,200 pounds. The cow eats more than 20 pounds of grass in a single day and drinks up to 30 gallons of water. Many ranchers depend on rain, snowmelt, and healthy pastures to feed and water their herds. Without enough water, the pastures do not have enough grass to feed the herds.

Some ranchers buy hay, which is expensive. And the larger the area affected by a drought, the harder it is to find additional sources of hay. If they can't feed their herds, ranchers must cull or sell some of the animals.

On his ranch near Rio Vista, California, rancher Ryan Mahoney raises Angus beef cattle. The current drought is like nothing he or his family has seen in decades.

Cows in New Zealand in 2013, feeding on winter food supplies to supplement the inadequate summer grazing

Credit: Dave Young (CC BY 2.0)

Normal rainfall in the area is 16 to 18 inches, but in 2021, Mahoney's ranch got only 3 to 5 inches of rain. The impact has been dramatic. Because of the drought conditions, Mahoney has been forced to sell off many of his cattle. Some are butchered, while others are sent to ranches in other parts of the country.

"We in agriculture deal with the effects of climate change right up front. We are going to be the first ones impacted," said Mahoney. "In the city, you get some hot days and nights, but you don't face it like you do when you're farming and you don't have any feed to feed your cows or a fire burns everything you have."

Climate change can also increase the number of parasites and diseases that affect livestock.

Read more about the effect of the California drought on cattle in this article.

Why are farmers the ones feeling the effects of climate change more than people in cities?

NatGeo drought ranchers

Many parasites and diseases that affect livestock thrive in warm, moist environments. As temperatures rise, some areas are experiencing earlier springs and warmer winters. This allows parasites and pathogens usually killed by colder temperatures to survive more easily and for longer periods. In areas experiencing increased precipitation, pathogens that live in wet, moist environments thrive.

CHANGE UNDER THE SEA

Do you eat fish? Approximately 3 billion people in the world rely on seafood as a primary source of protein in their diet. However, climate change is already disrupting this critical food source.

As the atmosphere warms, the ocean absorbs excess heat. The top meters of the ocean store as much heat as all of Earth's atmosphere! Since 1955, the oceans have absorbed more than 90 percent of the excess heat trapped in the atmosphere. Today's ocean is warmer than it has been since 1880, when people started keeping records of ocean temperatures.

If the ocean warms too much, the plants and animals that live in it are forced to adapt or die. To find cooler waters, many fish and shellfish are moving north.

CLIMATE CLUES

Some disease-causing pathogens can also cause health problems in people who eat contaminated fish.

People who rely on fishing and lobstering for income are worried what the changing climate will do for their businesses.

For example, in the northeastern United States, species such as the American lobster, red hake, and black sea bass have moved north by an average of 119 miles since the 1960s. The Chinook salmon, which typically lives in the Pacific Ocean off the California and Oregon coasts, is now swimming into Arctic waters.

How would you feel if someone moved into your house and started eating all your food and sleeping in your bed?

Sometimes, when a species moves to a new area, it must compete for food and other resources with other species already living there. When fish change where they live, it also affects those who fish. They must either follow the fish into new waters or try to catch a different type of fish.

The ocean absorbs 80 to 90 percent of the excess heat in the atmosphere from global warming.

Warming waters have also been linked to outbreaks of marine diseases. On the Atlantic coast, higher water temperatures have allowed an oyster parasite to spread farther north along the coast. In the Arctic Ocean, warming temperatures have led to more salmon disease outbreaks and dwindling numbers of the Yukon Chinook salmon.

ACIDIC OCEANS AFFECT MARINE ANIMALS

Increased carbon dioxide in the atmosphere is also making oceans more acidic. As carbon dioxide in the atmosphere increases, the ocean absorbs almost a third of it, changing the water's natural chemistry. The sea becomes more acidic. Today, ocean waters are about 30 percent more acidic than during the 1800s.

Mussels are ocean creatures that are affected by the ocean's increased acidity.

Increasing ocean acidity is a problem because it can weaken the shells of shellfish such as mussels, making them more vulnerable to predators. Acidity also disrupts the development of fish larvae and changes how fish use their sense of smell to find food and habitats and avoid predators.

Ocean acidification can disrupt entire marine ecosystems. As fish struggle, the world's food supply also suffers. It threatens food security for the billions of people who rely on fish and seafood for nutrients.

EARTH'S WATER CYCLE

Water is essential for life. Every organism on Earth relies on water. We cannot live without a clean, dependable supply of drinking water. We use water in farming, energy production, manufacturing, recreation, and other activities.

In many areas, climate change is causing the demand for water to rise. At the same time, the world's clean water supplies are shrinking.

CLIMATE CLUES

Volcanoes release steam into the atmosphere, which forms clouds as part of the water cycle.

Where does Earth's water come from? Earth's water is always moving in a process called the water cycle or the hydrologic cycle. Water moves in a continuous cycle below, on, and above Earth's surface. Water also constantly changes states from liquid to vapor (gas) to ice (solid) and back to liquid.

The water cycle

Heat energy from the sun causes water to evaporate into water vapor, which rises in the atmosphere and reaches cooler air. The cooler air causes the water vapor to condense and form water droplets and clouds.

ENERGY AT HOOVER DAM

Hoover Dam produces hydroelectric power from water in Lake Mead. Water flows through the dam and spins turbines. The water's force on the turbines generates electrical energy. The electricity produced at Hoover Dam powers communities in Nevada, Arizona, and southern California. As the water in Lake Mead drops, the electricity produced by Hoover Dam also drops. For every foot the lake's water level drops, the dam loses about six megawatts of capacity. That's enough to power approximately 4,500 to 6,000 average American homes. What does this tell you about the importance of water?

Air currents in the atmosphere move clouds around Earth. As the water droplets become heavy, they fall to Earth in liquid form as rain and snow.

In some areas, glaciers form from the buildup of snow and ice. The water cycle continues when the sun's heat causes the snow and ice to melt into water. Most of the melting snow and ice flows into rivers, oceans, and even the ground. Some ice evaporates directly back into the atmosphere.

When precipitation falls as rain, some of it flows into rivers, lakes, and oceans. Some rain soaks into the ground and becomes groundwater. Groundwater seeps into rivers and lakes. In some places, it flows to the surface as springs. Other times, groundwater flows deep underground and remains there for many years. Some groundwater is taken up by plants and released as water vapor from their leaves back into the atmosphere. Sometimes, groundwater flows into oceans, where the water cycle begins again.

So how does climate change affect Earth's water cycle?

Warmer temperatures cause water to evaporate faster. Less water is available in lakes, rivers, streams, reservoirs, and groundwater supplies. In some places, this evaporation causes the ground to become drier and results in shortages in water supplies. As more water vapor fills the atmosphere, some areas experience increased rain or snow.

SHRINKING WATER SUPPLIES

In some areas of the world, people are already experiencing water shortages. Warmer temperatures have led to less annual rainfall, less snowpack in the mountains, and earlier snowmelt.

The sinking water level at Lake Mead

In a usual year, snowpack in the mountains melts during the summer and flows into reservoirs. Earlier snowmelt changes the timing of water flow into reservoirs and other bodies of water. This change, coupled with increasing water demands brought about by population growth, is making less water available during the high-demand summer months.

In the western United States, more than 40 million people depend on Lake Powell and Lake Mead, two of the country's largest water reservoirs. Lake Powell is a manmade reservoir on the Colorado River in Utah and Arizona. Lake Mead is another manmade reservoir that sits on the Colorado River in Nevada and Arizona. As these regions experience several years of extreme drought, the water levels in both reservoirs are at historic lows in 2021.

CLIMATE CLUES

In 2020, hydroelectricity generation provided about 7.3 percent of total U.S. utility electricity generation. Most U.S. hydroelectricity generation occurs in only five states: Washington, California, Oregon, New York, and Alabama.

The ocean can absorb 1,000 times more heat than the atmosphere. Watch this video to learn more.

What does this tell you about the importance of the earth's oceans?

NASA oceans climate change

Lake Powell dropped to 3,554 feet in July 2021, the lowest level since it was first filled in the 1960s. At Lake Mead, the water dropped to its lowest level since the 1930s. By July 2021, it held only one-third of its capacity.

Similar dips have happened at reservoirs across the Western states. If reservoir water levels continue to decline, officials will be forced to cut the water supply to the communities that rely on it.

Water shortages already affect people who depend on reservoirs. In California, the San Luis Reservoir was at about 30 percent of its capacity in July 2021. Farmer Joe Del Bosque grows melons and other crops in California's Central Valley. He relies on water from the San Luis Reservoir to irrigate his crops. In 2021, he left about a third of his farmland unplanted—there was simply not enough water to plant crops. What might this mean to the food supply if there isn't enough water to plant crops?

WATER QUALITY SUFFERS

While some areas are dealing with a lack of rain and water shortages, other communities face problems triggered by too much rain. Heavy rains and snow overwhelm sewer systems and water treatment plants in the Northeast and the midwestern United States. Heavy rain also increases the runoff that flows into rivers and lakes. The runoff carries sediment, pollutants, trash, animal waste, and other contaminants into the water supply.

According to the EPA, polluted runoff is one of the greatest threats to clean water in the United States.

In July 2021, record-setting rains led to tens of millions of gallons of untreated sewage being released into the Merrimack River, which provides drinking water for several Massachusetts and New Hampshire communities. The untreated sewage and stormwater came from several water treatment systems located along the river.

When the systems became overwhelmed with heavy rains, the untreated sewage and stormwater overflowed into the river. Boaters reported smelly brown waters and large numbers of dead fish. Environmentalists warn that large and frequent sewage and stormwater overflows can create a health risk to people who get drinking water from the river, as well as those who use it for boating and swimming.

Around the world, scientists, farmers, and many other people are working hard to reduce the impact climate change will have on the world's food and water supplies.

Sustainable agriculture practices can reduce crop losses from extreme weather and rising temperatures, improve soil health, and reduce greenhouse gas emissions. Water conservation efforts at all levels help to preserve the water supply. With these efforts and more, people will be better prepared to protect our food and water supplies from Earth's changing climate.

KEY QUESTIONS

- **How important is the water cycle to the health of the planet?**
- **How are drought and flooding related?**

VOCAB LAB 

Write down what you think each word means. What root words can you find to help you? What does the context of the word tell you?

contaminant, **crops**, **graze**, **livestock**, **malnutrition**, **parasite, pathogen**, **reservoir**, **snowpack**, **sustainable**, and **yield**

Compare your definitions with those of your friends or classmates. Did you all come up with the same meanings? Turn to the text and glossary if you need help.

TEXT TO WORLD

Have you ever had to conserve water? What habits did you change?

Inquire & Investigate

WHAT HAPPENS TO SOIL IN A DROUGHT?

Droughts are periods of abnormally low precipitation that lead to a water shortage. Droughts can last for weeks, months, or years. Severe droughts damage crops, dry topsoil, and shrink lakes and rivers. When wind carries away the dry topsoil, it can create a dust storm. Dust storms carry away plant nutrients and affect cities and towns in their paths. Strong dust storms can knock over trees, bury equipment, and damage homes and buildings. In this activity, we'll look at what happens to soil in a drought and the problems it can cause.

Ideas for Supplies

- two 2-liter soda bottles
- scissors
- marker
- measuring cups
- dry potting soil
- water
- small balance or scale
- clear plastic wrap
- bright sunlight or a lamp

- **Clean and dry two empty soda bottles.** Carefully use scissors to horizontally cut the soda bottles in half.
- **Take the two bottom halves of the soda bottles and label one "DRY" and the other "WET."** Scoop 1 cup of potting soil into each container. Add ¼ cup of water to the "WET" container.
- **Weigh each container and record your measurements.** What does the container's weight tell you about the moisture of the soil in it? As the soil dries, what do you expect to happen to the weight?
- **Cover both containers with plastic wrap.** Place both containers under a bright lamp or in direct sunlight.
- **After five minutes, check the plastic wrap.** What do you see? After 15 minutes? What is happening?

Inquire & Investigate

- **Carefully remove the plastic wrap from each container.** Make sure not to let any condensation on the plastic drip into the containers.
- **Weigh the containers again and record the weights.** Move the containers away from the lamp or out of direct sunlight and leave them uncovered overnight. The next day, weigh the containers and record the weights.
- **Cover the containers with plastic wrap and put both containers in direct light again.** After 15 minutes, carefully remove the plastic wrap and weigh the containers.
- **Create a graph of the change in soil moisture through time.** How long do you think it will take for the soil in the wet container to have the same level of moisture as the soil in the dry container?

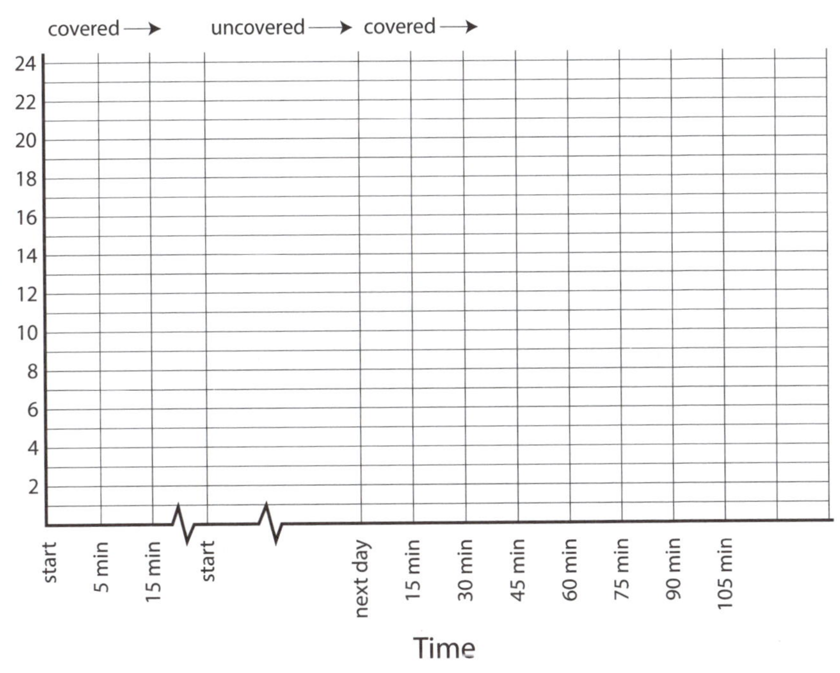

To investigate more, consider what happens when soil is exposed to wind. Does dry soil react differently than wet soil? Use a fan to test the reaction of each type of soil to wind. Under what conditions does the soil blow away?

Inquire & Investigate

HOW DO OCEANS ABSORB CARBON DIOXIDE?

Earth's oceans absorb carbon dioxide from the atmosphere. As greenhouse gases add more carbon dioxide to the atmosphere, the ocean also absorbs more of the gas. Why is this a problem? Increased amounts of carbon dioxide change the ocean's chemistry and make it more acidic. This can be harmful for the ocean's many ecosystems and affect the fish and shellfish that many people worldwide rely upon as an essential food source.

Carbon dioxide moves between the air and the ocean by a process called molecular diffusion. Molecules of carbon dioxide move from areas of higher pressure (air) to areas of lower pressure (water). When carbon dioxide gas moves into the ocean, it dissolves. How much dissolves depends on the salinity and temperature of the water. The colder the water, the more carbon dioxide can be dissolved. In this activity, we'll see how ocean temperature affects how well ocean water absorbs and dissolves carbon dioxide.

Ideas for Supplies

- safety goggles
- 3 bottles of seltzer water at room temperature
- 2 pots, large enough to hold seltzer bottles
- ice
- hot water
- towels for cleanup

- **Safety first!** Before you begin, put on the safety goggles. Make sure to do this activity in a place where it is okay to spill or spray water. Be careful not to point a bottle directly at a person or animal when you open it.
- **Place one seltzer bottle in a pot and surround it with an ice bath.** Place a second seltzer bottle in a pot filled with hot water. If you want, you can gently heat the pot and its contents on a stovetop. Leave the third seltzer bottle at room temperature.

- **Where is the carbon dioxide in each bottle?** What do you predict will happen when you open each bottle?
- **Start by opening the room temperature bottle.** What do you observe? Why does this happen?
- **Next, open the cold bottle.**
  - What happens this time?
  - How did what you observe differ from what happened with the room temperature bottle? Why?
- **Finally, open the warm bottle.**
  - What happens?
  - How was this bottle different from the other two? Why?
  - How does this demonstrate how temperature affects how much carbon dioxide can dissolve in the ocean?
- **Did you make a mess?** Use the towels to clean it up!

To investigate more, consider how the carbon dioxide affects the acidity of water. Use litmus paper test strips (you can buy online) to test the seltzer water. Compare your results to distilled water and tap water. What do you observe? What does that tell you about carbon dioxide and ocean acidity?

Chapter 3

Migration and Loss of Habitats

How does climate change alter habitats?

Climate change causes habitats to change, sometimes beyond what organisms can easily adapt to, causing them to migrate in an attempt to stay healthy.

In one way or another, every living organism feels the effects of climate change. Extreme weather, rising temperatures, water and food scarcity, and rising seas threaten habitats worldwide and endanger the species that live there.

Could you live in a place that didn't have any water or food? What about a place that was -100 degrees Fahrenheit (-73 degrees Celsius) year-round? Definitely not! That type of place would not be able to meet your survival needs. A thriving habitat must have the right mix of environmental conditions for an organism to survive.

HAVE SOME HABITAT

What makes a good habitat for one organism may not be good for another organism. For animals, a habitat must provide a source of food and water, a place to find a mate, and the right conditions to have offspring.

For plants, the right combination of sunlight, soil, air, and water is important. Some plants, such as cacti, grow in dry, sandy desert climates with bright sunlight. Other plants, such as moss, thrive in cool, wet, forested environments that receive limited sunlight.

The main elements of habitat are space, shelter, food, and water.

A tiny carpenter ant needs a small space to dig tunnels, find food, reproduce, and go about its activities. In comparison, a cougar roams more than 175 square miles when hunting or searching for a mate. The cougar would not be able to survive in the same tiny space as the ant.

Plants also need different amounts of space. Massive redwood trees can grow to more than 15 feet in diameter and 350 feet tall. A tree this size wouldn't be able to survive in an urban backyard! But a small rosebush may do well there.

A saguaro cactus in the Arizona desert

What about the food and water in a habitat? An American black bear typically eats roots, berries, grasses, succulent plants, insects, and meat. If the bear's habitat experiences a drought, plants may become hard to find and water sources could dry up. If the bear cannot find enough food or water, its habitat is no longer suitable.

Shelters protect organisms from weather and predators. Shelters can be anything from caves to underground burrows. Consider a tree—a bird may build a nest on a high branch in the tree, while an insect finds shelter under the tree's leaves. For a fungus, the cool, damp area near the tree's roots provides shelter.

Every organism lives in a specific habitat, with conditions suited to help it survive. When that habitat is lost or damaged, some species learn to adapt to the new conditions. Others are forced to migrate to new habitats. And some species find their survival in doubt.

HABITAT LOSS

Around the world, the effects of climate change—temperature changes, extreme precipitation, and rising sea levels—are already impacting habitats and the organisms that live in them.

In California, the ongoing drought is changing the habitats of much of the state's wildlife. Animals are forced to travel farther in search of water. Those that cannot adapt may not survive. For example, marshes are scattered through California's Mojave Desert. Various fish species have made these marshes their home. As the lack of rain causes the marshes to dry up, the fish habitat is being destroyed. Other animals and plants that rely on the marshes for water are also in trouble.

In California's forests, the death of millions of trees because of drought damages the forest habitat for many organisms. Small forest-dwelling animals depend on plants or plant products such as acorns for food. As the number of trees and plants declines, it becomes more difficult for these animals to find food. As the trees die, the canopy created by the treetops also shrinks. Without this cover, mice and rabbits living on the forest floor find it more difficult to hide from predators.

Some California species have traveled to new areas in search of fresh water and food sources. But when one species enters another species' habitat, the two must share the same limited resources. Sharing watering holes with new animals can spread disease. Some wildlife wanders into areas occupied by humans, causing clashes with their human neighbors. In California, black bear sightings in backyards and neighborhood trees are becoming more common as the animals leave their mountain habitat to search for food and water.

Climate change, as well as deforestation, is shrinking natural habitats worldwide. Approximately 18 percent of natural ranges, the areas where a species can be found in its lifetime, has already been lost. And a 2020 study predicts that habitat loss is expected to accelerate, with 23 percent of the world's natural habitat ranges lost by 2100. For species unable to adapt, this level of habitat loss could cause the rapid extinction of already vulnerable animals and plants.

Videos of wildlife eating at picnic tables and swimming in pools can be funny! Watch these bears taking a cooling dip.

What kinds of dangers can come of wildlife wandering into human living spaces?

bears swimming pool California

A RIPPLE EFFECT

When something affects one species in an ecosystem, it can have a ripple effect on every part of the ecosystem. California's Sonoran Desert is one example of this.

In the desert, drought conditions have led to desert plants dying at a high rate. According to scientists, native vegetation in the Southern California Sonoran Desert has declined by 37 percent during the past three decades. Usually, desert plants can withstand high heat and little rain. However, this drought's intense heat and arid conditions have pushed these plants to the limit. Scientists worry that if the region dries out even more, nothing will grow to replace the dying plants.

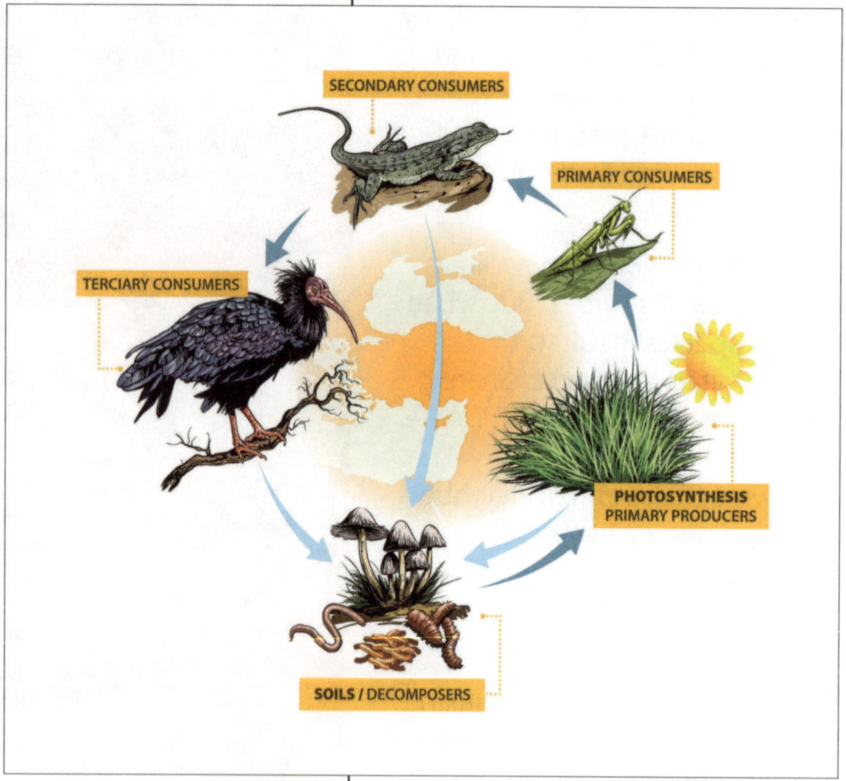

What happens when one of these elements of the food chain disappears?

Credit: Lukaves

As native vegetation dries up and dies because of habitat change, there is a cascading effect across the desert ecosystem.

Pollinator insects that depend on the vegetation no longer have a source of food and water. Lizards that eat the bugs face a dwindling food supply. Larger animals that prey on the lizards also struggle to find enough food. Some species that may already be endangered struggle even more to survive.

SPECIES ON THE MOVE

When faced with a changing climate and habitats, species must adapt or die. For many, the first response to a changing climate is to move to a new location.

Species migrate to escape increasing temperatures, rising sea levels, ocean acidification, and extreme weather. According to scientists, a survey of about 4,000 species worldwide revealed that about half are already moving to new areas. Many move toward the earth's poles or to higher elevations where they can find cooler temperatures.

Professor Gretta Peel at the University of Tasmania in Australia studies species migration due to climate change. She says that land-based species are moving toward the North and South Poles by an average of 10 miles per decade. In the world's oceans, marine species are moving toward the poles by an average of 45 miles per decade.

Some species are moving even faster. According to scientists at Plymouth University in the United Kingdom, the Atlantic cod and Europe's purple emperor butterfly have moved more than 125 miles in only 10 years! This type of mass migration of species is the largest in the past 25,000 years. The last time a mass migration of species occurred at this level was during the peak of an ice age.

Where a species will move is difficult to predict. Each species shifts at its own pace and responds differently to climate change. Some migrate because of changing temperatures, while others react to changes in precipitation or sunlight.

NEW PARTNERS

As species move to new habitats, they are suddenly living with new neighbors. Thrown together for the first time, some species are getting very close. They are interbreeding to create new, hybrid species. New, hybrid species of butterflies, sharks, toads, bears, and trout have appeared worldwide.

CLIMATE CLUES

Global warming is also moving the timing of some organisms' biological cycles. Some animals, such as frogs, other amphibians, birds, and butterflies, are reproducing earlier in the year. Some plants are flowering earlier in the spring as well. When these events shift earlier, it can have a ripple effect through an ecosystem.

CLIMATE CHANGE'S FIRST CASUALTY

For one species, it is already too late. The Bramble Cay melomys was a small rodent that lived on an island off the north coast of Queensland, Australia. It was the only mammal species native to Australia's Great Barrier Reef, visited by Europeans beginning in 1845. In 1978, scientists estimated that several hundred rodents lived on the island, but the melomys was last seen in 2009. In 2014, scientists searched extensively for the animal and never found it. The Bramble Cay melomys is considered the first mammal to be driven to extinction because of climate change. Researchers concluded that rising seas flooded the island multiple times, killing the rodents and destroying their habitat.

Species that do not migrate when faced with changing conditions may struggle to survive. In North America and Europe, the number of some bumblebee species is dropping. When scientists investigated, they discovered that bumblebees commonly found in the southernmost parts of their species' range have disappeared.

In North America and Europe, the bumblebee's southern range has moved north by 185 miles. At the same time, the bumblebees did not shift their northern range farther north, as other species such as butterflies and birds have done.

While scientists do not know why the bumblebees are not moving north, they suspect it may be linked to the bee's history.

Many other insects evolved in tropical climates and migrated to northern habitats. In contrast, bumblebees originated in cooler areas in the Northern Hemisphere. This difference may make them more resistant to migrating to escape warming temperatures. Scientists fear that this resistance to migration might eventually lead to the disappearance of the bumblebee.

SPECIES AT RISK

Climate change affects every species on Earth. Rising temperatures, changing precipitation patterns, rising seas, and extreme weather threaten Earth's habitats and the species that live in them.

Some scientists predict that nearly 50 percent of all the world's species could be in danger of extinction by 2100 if climate change continues unchecked. They expect that species living in the Amazon River basin, southern Africa, and southwest Australia will be the hardest hit. Let's look at some of the organisms in danger.

CLIMATE CLUES

Two-thirds of North American bird species face an increased risk of extinction because of warming global temperatures.

In North America, the monarch butterfly (*Danaus plexippus*) is a large butterfly with distinctive bright orange and black coloring. These insects are famous for their migration across North America to winter in southern regions. The monarch, like all butterflies, is very sensitive to changes in weather and climate. More frequent extreme weather events threaten the monarch's survival. Also, rising temperatures and frequent droughts make the butterfly's habitat drier and cause the loss of milkweed plants, upon which monarchs lay their eggs and rely on to feed their caterpillars. As a result of these changes, the monarch population is threatened.

Monarch butterflies and bumblebees are shifting their migration patterns because of climate change.

In Antarctica, the Adélie penguin (*Pygoscelis adeliae*) lives along the continent's coastline and on its small islands. This small penguin feeds mainly on krill, tiny crustaceans found in oceans.

An Adelie penguin feeding her chick

Warming air and ocean temperatures are already causing the Adélie penguin population to decline on the West Antarctic Peninsula. As temperatures rise, penguin chicks are finding it increasingly difficult to survive in coastal nesting grounds. In addition, warmer-than-usual ocean temperatures decrease the number of krill available as food for penguins.

DYING CORAL

Coral reefs are the most diverse marine ecosystems on Earth. Nearly 25 percent of all ocean species spend at least part of their lives on or near a coral reef under the ocean's surface. These species depend on coral reefs for food, shelter, and protection.

Corals are a type of marine animal. They use tiny tentacles to capture food from the surrounding water. A coral reef forms when many corals grow in one area. Coral reefs can take hundreds or thousands of years to fully develop. Corals require the right temperature, level of ocean acidity, and availability of light and nutrients to thrive. When those conditions change, corals become stressed. If the stressful conditions last, the corals begin to bleach, or turn white.

Sometimes, corals can recover from bleaching, but only if conditions improve quickly. If corals are bleached for a long time, they eventually die.

Learn more about coral reefs and coral bleaching in this video from the Great Barrier Marine Park.

What do the coral reefs need from humans right now?

Great Barrier Reef bleach 101

Climate change significantly affects coral reef ecosystems. Rising ocean temperatures create thermal stress on coral ecosystems, which contributes to bleaching. As CO_2 levels rise in the atmosphere, the ocean absorbs more CO_2, making the water more acidic. This decreases coral growth and weakens coral structures. Also, as storms such as hurricanes become stronger and more frequent, the ocean's coral reefs face a greater risk of destruction.

As temperatures rise, coral bleaching will become more common and severe. Coral reefs such as the Great Barrier Reef in Australia and the northwestern Hawaiian Islands in the United States have already experienced devastating bleaching. In 2016 and 2017, bleaching in the Great Barrier Reef killed about 50 percent of its corals. Scientists predict that more coral reef ecosystems will die if climate change continues at its current pace.

KOALAS AT RISK

In Australia, the koala (*Phascolarctos cinereus*) eats a particular diet—the leaves of the eucalyptus tree. Increasing levels of CO_2 in the atmosphere have caused nutrients in these leaves to decline. As a result, the koalas are not getting the nutrients they need, which leads to malnutrition and starvation. Plus, as drought conditions persist across the continent, fires are more likely to destroy the koala's forest habitat and many of the animals themselves. In dry conditions, koalas are forced to leave the safety of the trees to search for water and new habitats, which puts them in danger of predators and cars.

HUMAN MIGRATION

Climate change also drives people to rethink where they live. In a 2021 survey, 49 percent of people said they planned to move in the next year. Their reasons included extreme temperatures and increasing frequency and intensity of extreme weather.

Megan Warren grew up in Southern California and lived in Los Angeles for a decade and a half. In 2016, she realized that Los Angeles seemed to be constantly battling drought. Warren removed the dry, brown grass and other water-dependent landscaping from her yard and replaced them with succulents and ground cover better suited to dry conditions.

Every time Warren turned on the kitchen faucet, she worried about how much water she used. She dreamed of living in a place where she didn't have to worry about how long she took in the shower. When she explored the Pacific Northwest, it seemed like a dream. Water was plentiful, and trees and plants were green and lush. In 2016, Warren packed up her family and moved to Portland, Oregon.

She is one of a growing number of people around the world who are considering climate change when deciding where to live.

It's one thing to move from one North American state to another, but for some people, climate change has made their current way of life impossible. In 2019, Jorge knew that it was time to leave Guatemala. For five years, the country hardly ever saw rain. When it did rain, Jorge rushed to plant his last corn seeds. His hope surged when the corn seeds grew into healthy green stalks.

KOALA RESCUE

The International Fund for Animal Welfare (IFAW) partners with several local organizations to rescue and rehabilitate koalas in Australia. Veterinary clinics provide specialized care for injured koalas. Once injured koalas are ready for rehabilitation, they are released into safe, enclosed areas to relearn climbing and gain muscle strength. The IFAW partners also establish safe habitats where the koalas can be eventually released into the wild.

As ocean levels rise because of climate change, erosion threatens buildings too close to the beach, such as this site in Vietnam.

Then, without warning, a nearby river overflowed its banks, and Jorge's cornfields flooded chest-deep with water. After the flood, the rain stopped again. Everything died. Jorge knew that if he didn't move his family, they might die, too.

The weather patterns behind Jorge's troubles are expected to become more frequent as Earth warms. Many parts of Guatemala will soon become more like a desert. In some regions, rainfall is projected to decline by 60 percent. The water that replenishes streams and moistens soil will drop by as much as 83 percent. Researchers project that some staple crops will decrease by nearly a third by 2070.

Jorge and his family are just one example of people moving to survive. As Earth warms, hundreds of millions of people from Central America and Africa will be forced to move or starve.

Read more about climate refugees at this website.

What do you think are the biggest problems facing people who have to move because of climate change?

climate refugees

VOCAB LAB 

Write down what you think each word means. What root words can you find to help you? What does the context of the word tell you?

adapt, **coral reef**, **extinction**, **habitat**, **marine**, **marsh**, **offspring**, and **thermal stress**

Compare your definitions with those of your friends or classmates. Did you all come up with the same meanings? Turn to the text and glossary if you need help.

TEXT TO WORLD

Have you had to move because of climate change?

Climate change may trigger one of the biggest waves of global migration in Earth's history.

However, the good news is that local communities, governments, and research institutions are helping Earth's species prepare for climate change. Scientists are researching new and innovative ways to help species adapt to changing conditions. Global experts also use sophisticated computer modeling to identify actions that will help Earth's species thrive in a warmer world.

Several pilot programs to prepare vulnerable species for climate change are already in the field. In Tasmania, higher air temperatures have led to fewer chick-producing eggs for the shy albatross. Extreme rain and wind have also damaged their nests.

To help the albatross recover and adapt, scientists have installed artificial nests designed to increase offspring and offset the impact of climate change on these birds. So far, the program has been a success. The eggs laid in the artificial nests produced surviving chicks more than twice as often as eggs laid in naturally built nests.

Working together, we can help all of Earth's inhabitants adapt to our changing climate.

KEY QUESTIONS

- What are some challenges facing climate migrants?
- How might you help the planet and animal species in your region?

CLIMATE CHANGE IN YOUR BACKYARD

Every living thing on Earth feels the effects of climate change. That includes the living things in your backyard or a nearby park. In this activity, you'll investigate how climate change may impact the living things in your neighborhood.

- **Take a walk in your backyard or a local park.** What organisms live there? Make a list of everything you see in your science journal. What type of habitat do these plants and animals live in? What is the usual climate where you live?
- **Do some research to create a food chain/web for the ecosystem you observed.** Head to the library for help. What is the role of each organism in the ecosystem? What does each eat or what eats it?
- **Make a prediction about what will happen to your backyard ecosystem in the next 20 years.** Consider these questions to explain your reasoning.
  - How will climate change affect the plant and animal habitat?
  - How will rising temperatures affect the plants in your backyard ecosystem?
  - Do you think they will survive? Why or why not?
  - How will climate change affect the animals in the ecosystem?
  - Can these plants and animals adapt to a new climate?
  - Can they move to another, suitable habitat?

To investigate more, search for evidence in the backyard ecosystem that climate change is already affecting the organisms that live there. What evidence can you find? What impact has it had on the ecosystem?

Inquire & Investigate

CLIMATE REFUGEES

Climate change is a factor driving millions of people worldwide to move from their homes. These people, called climate refugees or environmental migrants, leave their home areas because of sudden and long-term changes to the environment. These changes include drought, extreme weather events, sea level rise, changes to seasonal weather patterns, and more. The changes threaten the people's health, security, well-being, and ability to earn a living.

- **To begin, learn more about climate refugees.** Read this 2021 article by the World Economic Forum.

World Economic Forum climate refugees

- **Select an area where people are leaving.** Consider the following in your research.
  - What was the usual climate in this area? How did people live there and make a living?
  - How has climate change affected this area? How have these changes in their climate affected the people who live there? Is it still a suitable habitat for the people who live there? Why or why not?
  - Why are people leaving the area? What threats do they face because of climate change? Is there an alternative to leaving? Where are they going?
  - What challenges do climate refugees or environmental migrants face?
- **Present what you have learned to your family, friends, or classmates.**

To investigate more, consider what adaptations would be needed for residents to remain in the area you chose to research. Under what circumstances would adaptation be possible?

Chapter 4

Rising Sea Levels

Why should we be concerned about rising sea levels?

As sea levels rise, flooding increasingly affects coastal communities, and the health of certain ecosystems is threatened.

In the Seaport District of Boston, Massachusetts, business is booming. General Electric is building a new headquarters, Amazon is hiring thousands of new workers, and Reebok recently opened a new office. Other companies, trendy restaurants, and apartment buildings are also making the Seaport District their home.

But after bad flooding in the winter of 2018, some people wonder about the future of a manmade peninsula that is barely above sea level. Greg Hoffmeister watched the 2018 flooding from his third-floor Seaport office. "That was the first winter where we really saw waves splashing onto the boardwalk and water in the streets. You start to think: Is that what we're in for as sea levels rise?" he said.

Experts are not surprised. In 2020, the National Oceanic and Atmospheric Administration (NOAA) reported Boston had more sunny-day flooding than nearly any other U.S. coastal community.

NOAA defines sunny-day flooding, also called high-tide flooding, as water rising about two feet above the typical daily high-tide level. The flooding damages homes, destroys roads, and threatens water and sewer systems.

As sea levels rise, floods that used to happen only during storms now occur more regularly on non-stormy days because of a change in wind or currents or during a full moon.

Read more about sunny-day flooding in this article.

How is this different from floods caused by severe storms?

NPR rising tide more flooding

All that water in Boston Harbor has to go somewhere when sea levels rise.

According to the 2020 NOAA report, U.S. coastal communities saw an average of four days of sunny-day flooding in 2019. Boston experienced seven days in 2019. And the experts expect the flooding to get worse as sea levels rise.

NOAA scientists project that in a decade, Boston may experience as many as 35 days of sunny-day flooding. By 2050, the city could be flooded up to 95 days per year. "We know the water is going to be coming in through South Boston, pretty much from every direction, by 2070," said Richard McGuinness, a city planning deputy, referring to the neighborhood that includes the Seaport.

According to NOAA, coastal communities around the country are setting records for sunny-day flooding. In Boston, the record for sunny-day flooding occurred in 2017, when high tides flowed into parts of the city on 22 days. Charleston, South Carolina, experienced 13 days of flooding in 2019, compared to two days in 2000. In Texas, a community near Galveston Bay called Eagle Point experienced 64 days of flooding in 2019, compared to zero days in 2000.

On average, scientists predict that coastal communities will experience 25 to 75 days of sunny-day flooding by 2050.

Some communities face an even more significant threat. By 2050, flooding could impact Grand Isle, Louisiana, as many as 270 days per year.

CLIMATE CLUES

Tides are the regular rise and fall of the ocean's level. Tides are caused by the gravitational forces between the earth, the moon, and the sun. Ocean tides rise and fall as the moon rotates around the earth and the sun's position changes.

WHAT IS CAUSING RISING TIDES?

Just looking at the ocean, it's hard to tell that it is rising. Sea levels rise slowly. But with satellite and tide data, scientists know that sea level is rising about 0.13 inches per year, a rate that is increasing. According to Josh Willis, an oceanographer and climate scientist at NASA, global warming adds about 750 gigatons of water to the ocean each year. That's enough water to cover Texas in more than 3 feet of water.

For centuries, global sea levels changed very little. According to NOAA, however, since 1880, sea levels have risen by about 8 to 9 inches. A third of the increase occurred in the last two and half decades.

Global warming causes sea levels to rise in two main ways. First, warming causes glaciers and ice sheets near the poles to melt, which adds water to the world's oceans. Mountain glaciers usually melt a little every summer. Winter snows made up of evaporated seawater replenish the glaciers. As temperatures rise, however, more melting occurs in the summer, and less snow falls in the winter.

This imbalance adds more water to the oceans and causes sea levels to rise. Warming also melts the massive ice sheets that cover Greenland, adding water to the oceans.

CLIMATE CLUES

Ice sheets will keep melting for hundreds to thousands of years, according to a 2021 United Nations report. The melting will cause sea levels to continue rising beyond 2100 and stay high for thousands of years, even as we work to solve the climate crisis.

Second, as Earth's atmosphere warms, the ocean absorbs more of the increased atmospheric heat, and ocean water temperatures rise. As ocean temperatures rise, the ocean water expands and takes up more space, and sea levels rise.

The Arctic is warming more than twice as fast as the rest of Earth.

Other factors can cause changes in sea levels. For example, sediment accumulation occurs when ocean currents carry and deposit sediment on the ocean floor and build it up. Natural geologic activity such as an earthquake can cause land to rise vertically. Other times, land sinks due to erosion or sediment compaction. Changes in ocean currents can also impact sea levels by pushing more water against some coastlines and pulling it away from other coastal areas.

Watch the science behind melting glaciers in this video.

How does climate change contribute to the loss of glaciers?

NASA glacier melts

WHY DO WE CARE ABOUT SEA LEVEL?

As Earth's atmosphere and oceans continue warming, sea levels are expected to rise for many years. In the coming years, scientists project that sea-level rise will occur at an even faster rate. What does that mean for you?

Many people live in coastal areas, where sea level is a factor in flooding, erosion, and storm hazards. Rising seas threaten roads, bridges, subways, water supplies, oil and gas wells, power plants, and more. Damage to essential infrastructure can cripple businesses, industries, and jobs.

Higher sea levels also mean storm surges will move farther inland and damage more areas when intense coastal storms hit. Storm surge occurs when a strong storm causes ocean water to rise above normal tide levels. The water moves inland and floods coastal communities. Often, storm surge causes significant damage and can be deadly. Even without a storm, higher sea levels will lead to more frequent high-tide flooding in some areas, which can be very destructive and costly.

ERODING SHORELINES

Ocean Isle Beach is a small seaside resort town on the southern coast of North Carolina. It is located on a 5-mile barrier island. The Atlantic Intracoastal Waterway and marsh savannahs separate the island community from the mainland.

A walk on the beach reveals the battle between the town and rising seas. Along the shore, residents have piled giant sandbags to protect homes from the encroaching sea. Some homes sit on stilts above the waves during high tide. Other homes that used to have two streets of houses between them and the sea are now oceanfront properties.

Through the years, a significant amount of coastal erosion has impacted the eastern end of Ocean Isle Beach. Sea level around the community has risen about 3 inches since the early 1980s. As the sea has risen, it has eaten away at the coastline and caused the beach to erode. Because of the beach erosion and rising sea, homes along the shoreline became more vulnerable to flooding. Several houses have been lost.

CLIMATE CLUES

Almost 40 percent of the U.S. population lives in coastal areas and eight of the world's 10 largest cities are near a coast.

MEASURING SEA LEVEL

Scientists measure sea levels using tidal stations and satellite laser altimeters. A tidal station is a location where tidal measurements and observations are made. Around the world, tidal stations tell scientists what is happening to the sea level at those locations. Scientists measure the water's height relative to a particular point on land. And to measure the average height of the entire ocean, scientists use satellite laser altimeters—instruments operated from a plane, helicopter, or satellite that provide information about the surface or topography of the planet. Scientists use all this data to understand how sea levels are changing through time.

Erosion on Ocean Isle Beach

Credit: Justin Champion (CC BY SA 3.0)

Beach erosion is a problem facing many coastal communities around the world.

Every inch of sea-level rise currently causes about 100 inches of beach loss.

Erosion is a natural process during which water and wind remove sand and soil from beaches. Erosion can cause a beach to lose several feet of sand each year. Although intense storms and hurricanes can cause sudden and rapid beach erosion, many communities are fighting chronic erosion. This is affected by the relative sea level—the height of the ocean relative to the land—and the supply of sand on a beach.

As sea levels rise faster, the natural process of coastal erosion will accelerate and become worse. While flooding typically happens from time to time, sea level rise allows waters to gradually overtake natural barriers such as wetlands, mangrove forests, and salt-water marshes that protect coastlines from sea flooding. Rising seas have even overcome manmade barriers built to protect coastal areas. Communities that were protected from flooding are devastated by water.

A growing number of coastal cities are taking action against rising seas. Some are building sea walls and surge barriers and installing water pumps and overflow chambers to keep water out. Some are restoring mangroves and wetlands to help lessen floodwaters. And some cities are re-thinking their urban design to incorporate water-friendly features such as parks and greenspace to protect the cities from flooding.

LOSS OF WETLANDS AND MARSHES

Around the world, wetlands are a vital part of the environment. In a wetland, water is present at or near the soil's surface year-round or for part of the year. Wetlands can be swamps, marshes, or bogs. Different types of wetlands have different soils and plants. The soil in swamps and marshes holds many minerals. Most of the plants in swamps are trees, while marshes have grassy plants. In bogs, the soil has few minerals. Mosses and a few other types of plants grow in bogs.

CLIMATE CLUES

Coastal erosion in the United States causes property losses of about a half-billion dollars each year.

LIVING WITH WATER

Some cities have turned to a Dutch concept known as "living with water" to protect themselves from coastal flooding. Instead of building walls and barriers to keep the water out, cities are creating plans to direct the water where it will do the least amount of damage. In Boston, Massachusetts, city planners are developing a system of waterfront parks and greenspaces along the coast. They are also elevating high-risk flood areas, raising streets, and building barriers. City planners believe the new waterfront design could absorb at least 21 inches of sea-level rise and keep the city safe from unwanted flooding.

Take a look at this graph from the EPA that tracks global absolute sea-level change from 1880 to 2019.

What predictions can you make for the future?

EPA climate sea levels

Wetlands play an essential role in the environment. They provide food, shelter, and protection for many types of plants and animals. Wetlands also filter water and absorb excess nutrients, sediment, and pollution before they reach lakes, rivers, and other bodies of water. During excessive rain, coastal wetlands act as a natural barrier to protect shorelines by absorbing and slowing floodwaters before they reach communities. In the United States, coastal wetlands exist along the Atlantic, Pacific, Gulf, and Alaskan coasts.

Rising sea levels threaten coastal wetlands because they allow more ocean water to flow into the wetlands.

Wetlands have a specific water tolerance. If the water is not deep enough, the area is not a wetland. If the water becomes too deep and covers the soil and vegetation, the wetland slowly becomes an area of open water.

Usually, wetlands adapt to changing sea levels. Wetland plants trap sediment in a process called accretion, which increases the wetland's elevation. However, sea levels are projected to rise because of climate change faster than the wetland's natural accretion process. The rising seas would overrun the wetlands.

CLIMATE CLUES

Wetlands are the world's most biologically diverse ecosystems. They provide habitats for more than 19,500 animal and plant species worldwide.

To survive, some wetlands located on gently sloping land could slowly shift to a higher elevation. Yet many communities have built houses in these areas along the coast, leaving little room for the wetlands to adapt.

Scientists predict that 20 to 90 percent of today's coastal wetlands could be lost by 2100 because of rising seas.

The loss of wetlands would destroy valuable habitats for many species. No longer protected by wetlands, communities would be more vulnerable to coastal flooding and damaging storm surges. And Earth would also lose an important way to reduce carbon in the atmosphere, as wetlands trap large amounts of carbon.

SHRINKING COASTAL LOUISIANA

In Louisiana, scientists predict rising seas will likely overrun the coastal wetlands that line the Louisiana coast and protect New Orleans from flooding. During hurricanes, the wetlands absorb and weaken storm surges and protect the city. If sea levels rise more than 0.2 to 0.35 inches per year, the Louisiana wetlands could be flooded by ocean water by 2070. Coastal Louisiana is already losing land at a concerning rate because of a combination of rising sea levels and sinking land. Twenty-five percent of the land that existed in the region in 1900 has disappeared under the water. Look at this news video to learn more about Louisiana's battle with coastal erosion.

KATC fading away

SALT-WATER INTRUSION

Beneath Earth's surface, groundwater fills empty spaces, holes, and cracks in underground rock layers. Humans extract groundwater using water wells. Precipitation, snowmelt, and water from lakes and rivers naturally replace groundwater. The amount of water stored underground depends on an area's geography, how much water is taken out, and how the groundwater is replaced.

CLIMATE CLUES

Forty-four percent of the U.S. population relies on groundwater to supply clean drinking water.

Along the coasts, groundwater and salt water meet and mix in underground transition areas. Most of the time, groundwater's natural movement toward the sea prevents salt water from entering freshwater supplies. However, a combination of sea level rise and taking out too much groundwater can cause salt water to move into fresh water.

When people remove too much groundwater, salt water can make its way into fresh water supplies in a process called salt water intrusion.

Groundwater pumping reduces the fresh-water flow toward the coast. As the fresh-water flow and pressure lessen, seawater meets less resistance and moves more easily inland toward fresh-water supplies. Also, as the sea level rises, the amount of salt water entering the groundwater supply increases. In some cases, this affects water quality and makes it too salty to drink or use. In extreme cases, a groundwater well will need to be abandoned.

COASTAL AQUIFERS

Globally, coastal aquifers supply fresh water for drinking, irrigating crops, bathing, and other uses to more than 1 billion people living in coastal regions. An aquifer is a collection of wet, underground rocks, sand, and stones with small holes and cracks throughout them. These tiny openings allow the water to move through the rock slowly. For an aquifer to work, the rock, sand, and stones must be permeable so water can pass through. Aquifers often consist of permeable rocks such as sandstone or loose materials such as sand. Some aquifers consist of more dense rock with cracks or holes where water can pass through.

Salt-water intrusion along Alligator River in North Carolina

Coastal communities are already dealing with salt-water intrusion and the problems it causes. As sea water moves inland underground, it threatens water supplies, farming, and ecosystems. Research reveals that seawater increasingly threatens water supplies from private wells and public aquifers from New York to Florida along the East Coast.

Some underground fresh-water sources are already as salty as seawater. In South Florida, almost one-third of 215 monitoring wells reported increasing salinity during five years. Only 16 wells showed a downward trend in salinity.

VOCAB LAB 

Write down what you think each word means. What root words can you find to help you? What does the context of the word tell you?

aquifer, **current**, **erosion**, **geologic**, **high tide**, **salt-water intrusion**, **storm surge**, and **wetland**

Compare your definitions with those of your friends or classmates. Did you all come up with the same meanings? Turn to the text and glossary if you need help.

TEXT TO WORLD

Do you live in a coastal area? Is your region taking steps to deal with rising sea levels?

As salt water moves inland above and below the ground, once green forests along the U.S. East Coast die off. Ghost forests filled with bleached-white dead and dying trees are spreading along the coast.

Salt-water intrusion also threatens inland communities. In California's Central Valley, critical water supplies are threatened by salt-water intrusion from the Sacramento-San Joaquin Delta.

Because of the decreased water supply, California farmers may have to let 500,000 to 1 million acres of farmland go unplanted during the next 20 years. If the aquifers are not replenished, the Central Valley's many farms may go dry permanently.

California is the largest agricultural producer in the United States and provides two-thirds of its fruits and nuts and more than one-third of its vegetables.

How far the world's oceans will rise will depend on what we do in the coming decades. If countries can work together and take action to sharply reduce greenhouse gas emissions that are contributing to Earth's warming temperatures and warming seas, we may be able to improve the lives of the millions of people who live in coastal communities worldwide.

KEY QUESTIONS

- **How is the problem of rising sea levels different for islands? For regions on large continents?**
- **Why are wetlands important?**

MELTING ICE AND RISING SEAS

Melting ice contributes to sea-level rise because it adds more water into oceans. As Earth's temperatures rise, its glaciers and ice sheets are melting faster than they can be replenished with new snow and ice. The melting ice runs into the ocean. Let's model this process.

- **Divide the modeling clay into two equal amounts.** Press one-half of the clay into one side of one food container to create a smooth, flat continent rising out of the ocean. Repeat in the other plastic container.
- **In one container, add as many ice cubes as can fit onto the flat clay surface to represent glaciers on land.** In the second container, add the same number of ice cubes to the bottom of the tub to represent icebergs and frozen seawater.
- **Add water to the iceberg container so that the ice cubes float and do not sit on the container bottom.** The water should not rise above the land (clay) level.
- **In the glacier container, add water until the water level is about the same as the water level in the iceberg container.** Make sure not to disturb the ice cube glaciers on land. Use a marker to mark the water level on the container.
- **What happens in the containers?** Compare the water level with the original mark on the container. What do you notice? Repeat your measurements several times until the ice in both tubs is completely melted. Did the water level rise more in the glacier or iceberg container? How does this demonstration relate to sea-level rise?

Inquire & Investigate

Ideas for Supplies

- modeling clay
- 2 medium-sized clear, disposable food containers
- ice cubes
- water

To investigate more, consider what other ripple effects melting glaciers, ice sheets, and seawater ice have on Earth and its ecosystems.

Inquire & Investigate

COASTAL EROSION

The world's beaches are an important natural resource. But beaches are losing sand each year because of erosion, rising sea levels, and intense storms. Let's see how coastal erosion works.

Ideas for Supplies

- large, rectangular clear plastic container (disposable food container)
- metric ruler
- several different color markers
- sand
- water
- food coloring (optional)
- toothpicks

- **Use a ruler to make a mark at each centimeter along the longer side of the rectangular container.**
- **Add sand to the container so that it covers the bottom.** Push the sand to one end of the container so that it forms a sloping beach.
- **Add water to the container to cover the bottom and some of the sand.** Leave at least two inches of sand above the water line to represent a beach. You can add a few drops of food coloring to the water to help you see it better.
- **On the outside of the container, trace the slope of the beach with a marker.** Make a small mark on the outside of the container where the water and sand meet. Inside the container, use toothpicks to mark where the beach sand meets the water. Measure the different parts of the beach and record your data.
- **To create waves, carefully lift the ocean end of the container about 1 inch off the table and put it back down 20 times.** What happens? On the side of the container, use a different color marker to trace the line of the sloping beach and mark the shoreline. How has the beach changed?
- **Move the sand to restore the original beach slope.** Create more intense waves by lifting the container a little higher this time. Repeat 20 times.

- **Use a different color marker to trace the line of the sloping beach and mark the shoreline.** How did the more intense waves affect the beach?
- **Move the sand back to the original beach slope once more.** Add a little more water to the container to simulate rising sea level. Mark the new shoreline. Create the original size waves by lifting the container 1 inch off the table. Trace the changing beach slope and shoreline. What happens to the beach?

To investigate more, think about ways to slow coastal erosion. Design a seawall or other structure to preserve the beach. Using materials you can find around your house, build and test your design. How successful is it at preventing coastal erosion?

Chapter 5

Disease and Human Health

How does climate change threaten human health?

Extreme weather events and increasing temperatures can cause disease and death in several different ways. By being prepared and knowing what to look for, you can stay safe and help others.

In June 2021, Geoffrey-Martin Cyr lounged by the pool in Palm Springs, California. The 55-year-old Cyr was visiting the vacation town in the Sonoran Desert of Southern California for the weekend. That afternoon, Cyr stayed outside for more than an hour as the temperature reached 119 degrees Fahrenheit (48 degrees Celsius), making it one of the hottest days of the year in Palm Springs. It was so hot that Palm Springs resident Jill Langham, Cyr's friend, said the soles of her sneakers melted.

Langham and Cyr planned to meet later in the day, but Cyr never made it. On the way to the restaurant, Cyr vomited several times and collapsed on the street. Paramedics rushed Cyr to the hospital. His body temperature soared to 105 degrees Fahrenheit. His organs began to fail, and his blood pressure dropped from severe heatstroke. Despite the efforts of medical staff, Cyr died the next day.

According to climate scientists with the Union of Concerned Scientists, extreme heat such as Cyr experienced is one of the top weather-related causes of death in the United States. Heatstroke happens when your body overheats. Your body temperature can rise to 104 degrees or more in as little as 10 to 15 minutes. Without emergency treatment, a body temperature that high can cause permanent disability or death.

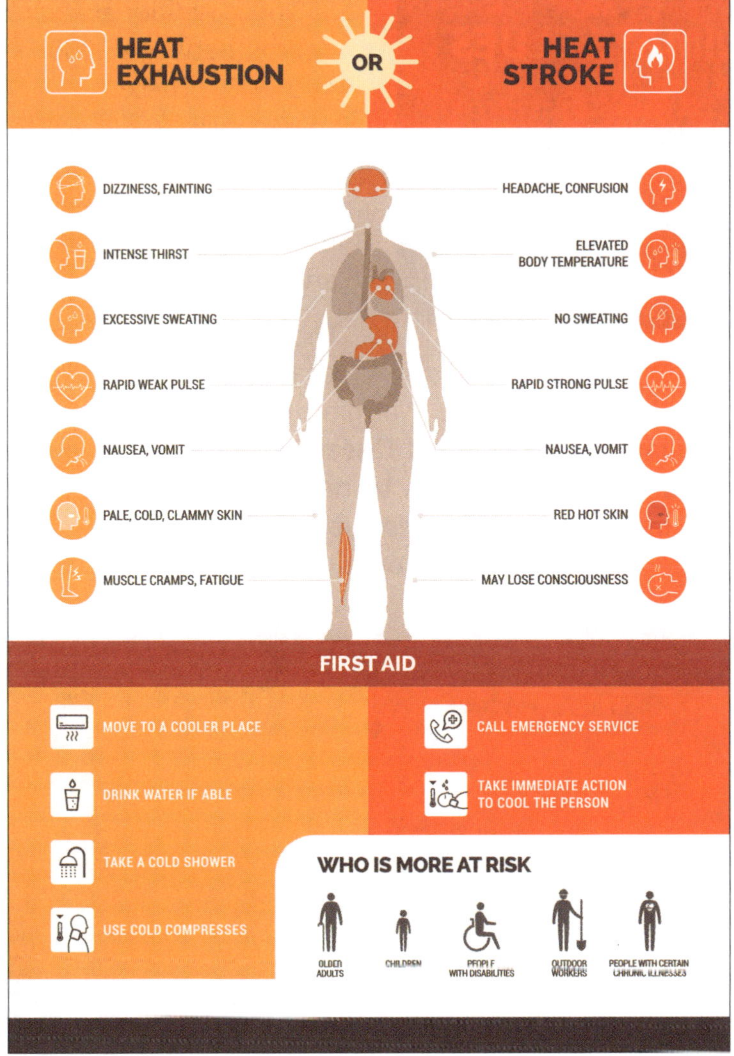

HEAT-RELATED ILLNESSES

Exposure to extreme heat and humidity without drinking enough fluids can cause heat-related illness. Heat cramps are the mildest form of heat illness. During high heat, your muscles will often painfully cramp and spasm after exercise and sweating. Heat exhaustion occurs when you lose water and salt from heat and sweating and they are not adequately replaced. Your body cannot cool itself properly. If untreated, heat exhaustion can become heatstroke, the most severe form of heat illness. Excessive heat overwhelms your body and it cannot regulate its temperature. Apart from high body temperature, symptoms of heatstroke include nausea and vomiting, rapid breathing, racing heartbeat, headache, confusion, and flushed skin. If you suspect heatstroke, seek immediate medical attention.

URBAN HEAT ISLAND

Have you ever noticed that it feels hotter in a city than it does in the country? It's not your imagination! Urban areas are usually hotter than rural areas. The difference in temperature occurs because of the way surfaces in each environment absorb and hold heat. Rural areas are often filled with grass, plants, and trees. The plants release water vapor into the air in a process called transpiration. It naturally cools the air. Most cities are full of sidewalks, streets, parking lots, and buildings made from cement, asphalt, brick, glass, and steel. These materials are often dark in color and absorb light energy from the sun and convert it to heat. A sidewalk in the sun feels much hotter than a patch of grass right next to it.

THREAT TO HUMAN HEALTH

Cyr's death from extreme heat is one example of how climate change and its effects threaten human health worldwide. The impacts of climate change affect the food we eat, the water we drink, the air we breathe, and the weather in our communities. Researchers with the World Health Organization (WHO) predict that the effects of climate change will contribute to about 250,000 additional deaths between 2030 and 2050. These deaths will be linked to conditions such as heat-related illnesses, malnutrition, diarrhea, and malaria.

CLIMATE CLUES

In dry, hot cities such as Phoenix, Arizona, adding trees and green space can reduce the urban heat island effect. This can also reduce pollution and provide recreation benefits for city residents.

The effects of climate change can also create new health problems. Warming temperatures and habitat loss may spread disease-carrying insects such as mosquitoes and ticks to new areas. As they move, the insects carry diseases such as West Nile virus or Lyme disease to new groups of people.

Deer ticks can spread Lyme disease.

CHANGING TEMPERATURES, ILLNESS, AND DEATH

As we've discussed, Earth has been warming during the past century. Average temperatures have increased and heatwaves are more frequent and severe. Extreme cold is less common. And the heat is projected to keep rising.

Scientists project average U.S. temperatures will increase by 3 to 10 degrees Fahrenheit (1.5 to 6 degrees Celsius) by 2100.

Rising temperatures have a direct effect on human health. Extremely hot or cold days make it harder for the human body to regulate its temperature. When the body cannot control its internal temperature, a variety of illnesses can occur. Heat-related illnesses include dehydration, heat cramps, heat exhaustion, heatstroke, and hyperthermia. When the body cannot regulate its temperature during extreme cold, you can suffer from hypothermia or frostbite.

Temperature extremes, particularly extreme heat, can also make existing conditions worse. People with cardiovascular disease, respiratory disease, or diabetes may find their health worsening. According to several studies, even slight differences in average temperatures can increase chances of illness and death.

CLIMATE CLUES

During the past century, air conditioning has become more common in homes and other buildings. This is bad news for the environment, but essential for health during heat waves! Air conditioners use a lot of power and result in CO_2 being released into the atmosphere—the very thing that is helping drive temperatures higher. Can you think of some possible solutions?

Read more about cooling centers in this article.

Why are they essential during a heatwave?

Health cooling centers

Migrant laborers work a strawberry farm in Canada in the heat.

TOLERATE THE HEAT

People are getting used to heat and learning how to live more safely with it. Communities respond to heatwaves by reaching out and checking on vulnerable, isolated citizens before they become seriously ill. Also, after repeated exposures to heat, the body can become acclimated and better able to handle high temperatures.

Some people are at higher risk of heat-related illnesses. Older adults and children are more likely to become seriously ill or die because of extreme heat because they are less able to regulate body temperature. People who work outside are more exposed to extreme heat. People without air conditioning and those who live alone with little outside social contact are also at increased risk of health problems from the heat.

AIR QUALITY

Do you have trouble with allergies during the spring or fall? Climate change might make those allergies worse. Climate change can worsen air quality and make air less healthy to breathe.

Higher temperatures can lead to an increase in allergens in the air. In higher temperatures, plants produce more pollen for longer periods. When inhaled, pollens from trees, grasses, weeds, and molds can trigger an allergic reaction in some people—congestion, itchy and watery eyes, and itchy noses or throats.

Longer and more intense pollen seasons can make allergy symptoms worse and last longer.

Higher levels of CO_2 also make allergies worse. Carbon dioxide makes plants grow more, which leads to more pollen in the air. And more moisture from increased rain and flooding can increase allergy-triggering molds.

Neelu Tummala is an ear, nose, and throat doctor in Washington, D.C. She sees many patients with allergy symptoms such as inflamed nasal passages, congestion, and postnasal drip. Dr. Tummala has noticed pollen seasons getting worse for her patients. Before, tree pollens occurred in the spring, grass pollens emerged in the summer, and ragweed pollen was common in the fall.

Now, the seasons have become longer and are starting to overlap. Some people who used to experience minor seasonal allergies are dealing with year-round congestion, sinus pain, and ear pressure.

Higher temperatures linked to climate change can also increase air pollutants, such as ground-level ozone or fine particulates. Ozone is found in Earth's upper atmosphere and at ground level as the main component in smog. While ozone in the upper atmosphere protects Earth from the sun's ultraviolet rays, ground-level ozone is an irritating air pollutant. It forms when cars, power plants, refineries, chemical plants, and other sources release pollutants into the air.

CLIMATE CLUES

Asthma is a chronic lung disease that causes inflammation and airway closing or tightening. People with asthma can experience coughing and trouble breathing.

When you breathe in ground-level ozone, it can cause several health problems—chest pain, coughing, throat irritation, and congestion. Breathing ground-level ozone makes bronchitis, emphysema, and asthma worse. It can also reduce your lung function and inflame the lining of your lungs. If you repeatedly breathe in this harmful pollutant, it can permanently scar lung tissue and lead to an early death.

Wildfires are another danger to breathing. Wildfires produce several harmful air pollutants, including particulate matter. Winds spread the particulates for hundreds of miles. Particles from wildfire smoke are often so tiny that they can travel deep into your lungs. The smallest particles can even pass directly from the lungs into your bloodstream.

Smoke makes heart and lung disease worse, including asthma. In some cases, significant smoke exposure can lead to death.

Dr. Kristie Ross is a pediatrician at a children's asthma clinic in Cleveland, Ohio. Ross knows her clinic will be busy with patients when the weather turns hot and steamy. In such weather, air pollution from car and bus exhaust, coal-fired power plants, and other sources hover near Earth's surface. And the pollution makes it more difficult for her young asthma patients to breathe.

No matter where you live, climate change could worsen the air you breathe.

According to one study, ozone air pollution levels in the United States could rise 70 percent in the summertime by 2050. At this level of pollution, nearly all parts of the continental United States will have at least a few summer days with unhealthy air. For areas that already have many days with harmful ozone levels, we may have to deal with unhealthy air levels for most of the summer. Try to stay inside during peak ozone hours!

CLIMATE CLUES

Each year, air pollution kills about 7 million people, according to the World Health Organization. Climate change could make the health problem much worse.

THE RISK FROM EXTREME WEATHER

Earlier, we talked about the ways climate change affects weather around the world. Specifically, we looked at how Earth's changing climate makes extreme weather events more frequent and intense.

CLIMATE CHANGE AND MENTAL HEALTH

Not only should we pay attention to people's physical health, but also to the state of their emotions. Changes to our environment and physical health can also affect our mental health. Extreme weather events cause significant stress and can trigger mental health illnesses such as depression, anxiety, and post-traumatic stress disorder (PTSD). Plus, researchers have found that people with pre-existing mental health illnesses were three times more likely to die during a heatwave. One reason may be that some medications used to treat mental illnesses can make it more difficult for the body to regulate temperature.

Extreme weather events affect human health in several ways. Floods, hurricanes, and wildfires directly threaten the people in their paths. Extreme weather can also reduce access to safe food and drinking water. After power outages, reports of stomach and intestinal illnesses are common after power outages from people eating spoiled food and drinking contaminated water.

Damaged roads and bridges make it difficult to travel for medical help, medicines, and other treatment. Extreme weather can also disrupt phone and internet service, communications, and utilities.

Around the world, many people have already been injured or gotten sick during extreme weather events. Many others have lost their lives. In August 2017, Hurricane Harvey made landfall in Texas as a Category 4 hurricane. It threatened millions of residents with heavy rains, 130 mile-per-hour winds, and a massive storm surge that flooded coastal areas. The storm hovered over Texas for days, dumping more than 27 trillion gallons of rain across the state.

Flooding after Hurricane Harvey

With this enormous amount of rain, Harvey became the wettest Atlantic hurricane measured in history.

In some parts of Houston, more than 50 inches of rain fell. One-third of Houston was completely flooded. And the massive rain was so heavy that the entire city sank temporarily by almost an inch! In addition to causing about $125 billion in damage, Hurricane Harvey caused the death of more than 100 people. Some died directly from the storm, while others were killed indirectly in car accidents or from being unable to access medical services during the storm.

Sometimes, the response to extreme weather can put people's health and safety at risk. For example, emergency responders risk their lives to go into flooded areas, collapsed buildings, and fire-ravaged areas to save people. After an extreme weather event, many people are involved in disaster cleanup and rebuilding. These activities, which are necessary, can be risky. In some cases, they can lead to injury, illness, and even death.

Watch this news video about the daunting rescue and repair tasks for emergency responders after Hurricane Ida in Louisiana.

What dangers do they face?

NBC Grand Isle Ida

INSECTS AND DISEASE

Around the world, bloodsucking insects such as mosquitoes, ticks, and fleas transmit disease. When these insects bite an infected human or animal, they can acquire disease-causing microorganisms such as viruses, bacteria, and parasites from the infected person's or animal's blood.

The insect becomes a vector for disease. As the pathogen reproduces in the insect, the insect becomes infectious. When the infectious insect bites a healthy person, it passes the pathogen to the healthy person, which causes a new infection.

Often, an infectious insect can transmit the disease-producing pathogen in every bite for the rest of its lifespan. These diseases are called vector-borne diseases.

A plague victim in bed pointing out to three physicians the swell under his armpit, 1500

Ein vorred

Hie anfahen ist das büch genät liber pestilen

Als die altẽ wisen

Vector-borne diseases are often difficult to prevent and control. Few have effective vaccines to protect people from them. According to the WHO, vector-borne diseases cause more than 700,000 deaths per year. Some vector-borne diseases, such as the plague, have existed for centuries. Others were only recently discovered. Today some common vector-borne diseases include malaria, dengue, yellow fever, Lyme disease, West Nile virus, and Zika.

Vector-borne diseases commonly occur in tropical and subtropical regions, where conditions are ideal for disease-carrying insects to breed and thrive. However, changes in temperature and precipitation have increased where and how long the disease-carrying insects live.

These changes expose more people to vector-borne diseases and can cause sickness earlier in the year. For example, ticks that carry Lyme disease live only in areas that have the proper temperature. As temperatures rise, ticks can become active earlier in the season and can also expand into areas farther north.

CLIMATE CLUES

Every year, waterborne diseases affect hundreds of millions of people worldwide. Many of those sickened live in developing countries and do not have access to safe water.

FOOD SAFETY

Climate change also impacts the food we eat and its safety. You can become sick when you eat food contaminated with bacteria, viruses, or other microorganisms that can cause disease. You may also become ill from eating food that contains chemical contaminants. Contaminated food or beverages may cause fever, nausea, vomiting, stomach cramps, diarrhea, and other gastrointestinal problems.

While some people experience mild symptoms from foodborne infections, others can become very ill and even die.

According to estimates from the Centers for Disease Control and Prevention (CDC), one in six Americans gets sick from contaminated foods or beverages every year. Of those, approximately 128,000 become sick enough to be hospitalized and about 3,000 die. Anyone can get a foodborne infection, but people with weakened immune systems, pregnant women, young children, and the elderly have a higher risk of experiencing more severe illness.

WATERBORNE ILLNESS

Some infectious diseases, such as cholera, spread through contaminated water. Waterborne diseases are more common after severe rainfall or snowfall, which increase flooding and runoff and spread microscopic organisms, sewage, and other disease agents that contaminate water sources. Climate change that increases temperatures, precipitation, runoff, and flooding also increases the risk of waterborne illness.

CLIMATE CLUES

Extreme weather such as flooding and storms that damage roads and waterways can make it more difficult to distribute food safely.

VOCAB LAB 

Write down what you think each word means. What root words can you find to help you? What does the context of the word tell you?

allergen, **asthma**, **dehydration**, **particulate**, **respiratory**, and **vector**.

Compare your definitions with those of your friends or classmates. Did you all come up with the same meanings? Turn to the text and glossary if you need help.

Climate change and its effects make it more challenging to ensure what we eat and drink is safe. Higher temperatures linked to climate change provide an ideal environment for bacteria such as salmonella and listeria to grow more rapidly. And extreme weather events make it more likely that contaminants enter our food and water supplies. As a result, more people may become sick.

Climate change affects every living thing on Earth. The effects of human activities on Earth have set the wheels of climate change in motion. While the changes that have already occurred cannot be reversed in our lifetimes, actions that we take today may let us avoid devastating climate change in the future. And every little bit that we can do today for the planet may ensure a healthy future for the next generations of Earth's inhabitants.

From extreme weather events to rising sea levels, there is no doubt that climate change is here, and all living things on Earth are already feeling its impacts. However, there is some good news. Every day, more people, organizations, businesses, and governments are becoming engaged in protecting Earth and responding to climate crises. People worldwide are coming together to take action to change course on climate change. When we work together, we ensure humans and all living things may continue to find a home on Earth.

TEXT TO WORLD

Have you or someone you know had their health worsened by climate change?

KEY QUESTIONS

- **What is the connection between city planning and community health?**
- **What steps can you take to prepare for hotter temperatures in your town?**

HOW HEAT AFFECTS MOLD GROWTH

Mold is a type of fungus. Tiny mold cells called spores are in the air we breathe. When mold spores land on a suitable host, such as certain foods, they grow. Some types of mold are harmless, while others can be dangerous. Usually, eating food with mold is unsafe. Also, breathing mold spores can trigger allergies and cause other breathing and health problems. Rising temperatures, along with moisture from increased rain and flooding, can provide an ideal environment for mold. Let's look at how heat affects mold growth.

CAUTION: If you have mold allergies, skip this experiment.

- **Lightly spray each piece of bread with water.** Try to moisten the pieces the same amount. Place each slice of moistened bread in a sandwich bag and seal it. The bags will stay sealed for the entire experiment.
- **Label the bags with numbers.** Put bag 1 in the refrigerator, bag 2 at room temperature (not in direct sunlight), and bag 3 where it receives heat from direct sunlight. Keep the bags sealed!
- **The next day, examine each bag.** Can you see any mold growth? If you see mold, measure its size. Record your observations. Wash your hands every time you handle the bags.
- **Continue your daily observations and measurements for 10 days.** When you're finished, throw away the bags without opening them.
- **Use the data you have collected to create a graph.** What do your results show about the relationship between heat and mold growth?

Ideas for Supplies

- 3 slices of bread
- spray bottle of water
- 3 plastic sealable sandwich bags

To investigate more, repeat this experiment by varying the amount of moisture on each piece of bread to test the relationship between moisture and mold growth. Place each bag in the same place to keep the temperature constant. What do you observe?

GLOSSARY

absorb: to soak up a liquid or take in energy, heat, light, or sound.

accelerate: to change the speed of something through time.

acclimate: to adjust to a change in environment.

accretion: the gradual accumulation of layers of sediment.

accumulation: the acquisition or gradual gathering of something.

acidic: from acids, which are chemical compounds that taste sour, bitter, or tart.

activism: the policy or action of using strong campaigning to bring about political or social change.

adapt: to make a change to survive in new or different conditions.

agriculture: growing plants and raising animals for food and other products.

allergen: something that triggers an allergic reaction.

allergy: a condition in which the immune system reacts abnormally to a foreign substance.

altimeter: an instrument for measuring height above sea level.

anxiety: a feeling of fear or uneasiness about possible misfortune. In some cases, anxiety is a mental disorder.

aquifer: a layer of sand, gravel, and rock that has pores or openings through which groundwater flows.

arid: dry.

asthma: a respiratory condition marked by spasms in the bronchi of the lungs, causing difficulty in breathing.

atmosphere: a layer of gas surrounding Earth.

awareness: knowledge and understanding that something is happening or exists.

bacteria: microorganisms found in soil, water, plants, and animals that are sometimes harmful but often helpful.

beneficial: having good or helpful results.

biofuel: a fuel made from living matter, such as plants.

blood pressure: the pressure exerted by circulating blood on the walls of blood vessels.

bog: a marshy wetland made of decomposing plants.

breed: to produce offspring.

carbon dioxide (CO_2): a combination of carbon and oxygen that is formed by the burning of fossil fuels, the rotting of plants and animals, and the breathing out of animals or humans.

cardiovascular: related to the heart and blood vessels.

Celsius: a scale of measuring temperature.

chemistry: the study of the properties of substances and how they react with one another.

chronic: recurring.

climate: the average weather patterns in an area during a long period.

climate change: a change in long-term weather patterns, which happens through both natural and manmade processes.

climatologist: a scientist who studies and predicts general weather and climate during a long period of time and over a large area.

compaction: the process of crushing or compressing something so that it takes up less space.

condensation: the process of a gas cooling down and changing into a liquid.

congestion: a condition where nasal passages become swollen with excess fluid and mucus.

conservation: managing and protecting natural resources.

conserve: to save or protect something, or to use it carefully so it isn't used up.

contaminant: any pollutant or object that could harm a living organism.

contaminate: to pollute or make dirty.

coral bleaching: coral that turns white, indicating it is ill and dying.

coral reef: an underwater ecosystem that grows in warm ocean waters and is home to millions of creatures. Corals are tiny animals that build shells around themselves.

crops: plants grown for food and other uses.

crustacean: a group of marine animals that includes crabs, lobsters, shrimp, and barnacles.

cull: to remove animals from a group according to specific characteristics.

current: the steady flow of water or air in one direction.

cyclone: the name of a hurricane over the Indian Ocean, the Bay of Bengal, and Australia.

deforestation: the process through which forests are cleared to use land for other purposes.

dehydration: the dangerous loss of body fluids.

dense: packed tightly together.

depression: a common mental illness that causes a low mood and sadness.

diabetes: a disease that affects how the body uses blood sugar.

disease: a sickness that produces specific signs or symptoms.

dissolve: to mix with a liquid and become part of the liquid.

distribution: the way a product is divided up or shipped out to stores.

diverse: a large variety.

drought: a long period of unusually low rainfall that can harm plants, animals, and humans.

ecosystem: a community of living and nonliving things and their environment. Living things are plants, animals, and insects. Nonliving things are soil, rocks, and water.

elevation: a measurement of height above sea level.

emissions: something sent or given off, such as smoke, gas, heat, or light.

emit: to send or give out something, such as smoke, gas, heat, or light.

encroach: to advance into or enter a territory.

endangered: a species of plant or animal with a very low population that is at risk of disappearing entirely.

energy: the ability to do work or cause change.

erosion: the wearing away of a surface by wind, water, or other process.

evaporate: to change from a liquid to a gas, or vapor.

exosphere: a thin layer of gas surrounding a planet.

extinction: the death of an entire species so that it no longer exists.

extreme weather: weather that is far from what is normal for a specific place at a particular time of year.

factory: a large place where goods are made.

Fahrenheit: a scale for measuring temperature.

fertile: able to produce or reproduce.

flash flood: a sudden flood due to heavy rain.

food chain: a community of animals and plants where each is eaten by another higher up in the chain. Food chains combine into food webs.

fossil fuels: fuels made from the remains of plants and animals that lived millions of years ago. Coal, oil, and natural gas are fossil fuels.

frostbite: injury to body tissues caused by extreme cold.

fungus: a plant-like organism without leaves or flowers that grows on other plants or decaying material. Examples are mold, mildew, and mushrooms. Plural is fungi.

gastrointestinal: relating to the digestive system.

geologic: having to do with geology, the science of the history of Earth.

glacier: a huge mass of ice and snow.

global climate: a description of the climate of a planet as a whole.

GLOSSARY

global warming: a gradual increase in the average temperature of Earth's atmosphere and its oceans.

gravitational force: the force of gravity.

gravity: a force that pulls objects to the earth.

graze: to eat grass.

greenhouse effect: when gases in the atmosphere permit sunlight to pass through but then trap heat, causing the warming of the earth's surface.

greenhouse gases: gases such as water vapor, carbon dioxide, and methane that trap heat in the atmosphere and contribute to warming temperatures.

groundwater: water that is held underground in the soil or in cracks and crevices in rocks.

habitat: the natural home or environment surrounding an organism.

heat dome: created when an area of high pressure stays over the same area for days or even weeks, trapping very warm air underneath.

heat stress: a number of conditions where the body is under stress from overheating.

heat wave: a period of unusually hot weather that lasts for two or more days.

heatstroke: a condition during which the body gets dangerously overheated.

hectare: a metric unit of land equal to 107,000 square feet, or about 2½ acres.

high-pressure system: a clockwise flow of dry, sinking air that typically builds into a region behind a departing storm system.

high tide: the tide when the water is at its greatest elevation.

Homo sapiens: the Latin name for the genus and species of modern humans.

humidity: the amount of water vapor in the air.

hurricane: a severe tropical storm with winds greater than 74 miles per hour.

hybrid: something that combines two different things, such as a car that can use two different kinds of devices to power it. Also the offspring of two animals or plants of different species or varieties.

hydroelectric: energy from moving water converted to electricity.

hydrologic cycle: a continuous process of circulating water between Earth and its atmosphere through evaporation, condensation, and precipitation.

hyperthermia: an abnormally high body temperature caused by a failure of the heat-regulating mechanisms of the body.

hypothermia: a medical emergency that occurs when the body loses heat faster than it can produce heat, causing a dangerously low body temperature.

ice age: a time in history when much of Earth was covered in ice.

ice core: a sample of ice taken out of a glacier, used to study climate.

immune system: a system in your body that removes pathogens.

import: to bring in goods from another country in order to sell them.

Industrial Revolution: a period during the eighteenth and nineteenth centuries when large-scale production of goods began and large cities and factories began to replace small towns and farming.

industrialized: when there is a lot of manufacturing. Products are made by machines in large factories.

infestation: an abundance of pests.

infrastructure: the large-scale public systems, services, and facilities of a country or region, including power and water supplies, public transportation, telecommunications, roads, bridges, and schools.

insulate: to shield or protect from outside influences.

interbreeding: one species mating with another species to produce offspring.

irrigation: moving water through canals, ditches, or tunnels to water crops.

jargon: the technical terminology for a certain field.

krill: small crustaceans found in all the world's oceans.

landform: a physical feature of the earth's surface, such as a mountain or a valley.

larva: an organism at the beginning stage of development. Plural is larvae.

legume: a plant with seeds that grow in pods, such as peas and beans.

life cycle: the growth and changes a living thing goes through, from birth to death.

livestock: animals raised for food and other uses.

low-pressure system: a mass of warm, moist air with strong winds that spiral in toward a low-pressure center. Low-pressure systems generally bring stormy weather.

malaria: an infectious disease transmitted by mosquito bites.

malnutrition: poor nutrition caused by not eating the right foods.

mangrove: a tree or shrub that grows in tropical coastal swamps.

manufacture: to make something by machine in a large factory.

marine: having to do with the ocean.

marsh: an inland area of wet, low land.

mass produce: to manufacture large amounts of a product.

medical examiner: a medical official who investigates deaths and injuries in crimes.

megawatt: a unit of power.

mesosphere: the part of the atmosphere above the stratosphere but below the thermosphere.

meteorologist: a person who studies the science of weather and climate.

microorganism: an organism so small it can be seen only under a microscope.

migration: the movement of a large group of organisms, such as birds, due to changes in the environment.

mineral: a nutrient found in rocks and soil that keeps plants and animals healthy and growing.

mold: a furry growth of fungus.

molecule: a group of atoms, which are the smallest particles of an element, bound together.

nutrient: a substance in food and soil that living things need to live and grow.

nutrition: the vitamins, minerals, and other things in food that your body uses to stay healthy and grow.

offspring: an animal's young.

orbit: the path of an object, such as a planet circling another in space.

organism: a living thing, such as an animal or a plant.

ozone: a gas that is a major air pollutant in the lower atmosphere but a beneficial part of the upper atmosphere. The ozone layer blocks most ultraviolet solar rays.

paleoclimate record: Earth's past climates. By studying the paleoclimate record, scientists can better understand today's climate.

parasite: an organism that feeds on and lives in another organism.

parched: dried out.

parliament: in some governments, the group of people responsible for making laws.

particulate: tiny particles.

pathogen: a bacteria, virus, or other microorganism that can cause disease.

permeable: a substance that liquid (or gas) can flow through.

pest: a destructive insect or other animal that attacks crops, food, and livestock.

photosynthesis: the process plants use to turn sunlight, carbon dioxide, and water into food.

plague: a deadly infectious disease carried by rats and mice that can spread to humans.

GLOSSARY

polar vortex: a large region of cold, rotating air that encircles both of Earth's polar regions.

pollen: a fine, yellow powder produced by flowering plants. Pollen is spread around by the wind, birds, and insects and is needed by a flower to make a seed.

pollination: transferring pollen from the male part of a flower to the female part so that the flower can make seeds.

pollinator: an insect or other animal that transfers pollen from the male part of a flower to the female part of a flower.

pollutant: a substance that is harmful to the environment.

precipitation: falling moisture in the form of rain, sleet, snow, or hail.

predator: an animal that hunts and eats other animals.

protein: one of the basic building blocks of nutrition.

PTSD: post-traumatic stress disorder, a condition in which a person has difficulty recovering after experiencing or witnessing a terrifying event.

radiate: to spread outward.

radiation: energy transmitted in the form of rays, waves, or particles from a source, such as the sun.

refugee: a person who has been forced to leave their country to avoid war, persecution, or natural disaster.

regional climate: the climate of a specific area.

reproduce: to make something new, just like itself. To have babies.

reservoir: a manmade or natural lake used to store water for drinking and other uses.

resistant: not affected or harmed by something.

respiratory: having to do with breathing.

runoff: water that flows off the land into bodies of water.

salinity: the amount of salt in water.

salt-water intrusion: salt water making its way into fresh water.

satellite: an object that circles another object in space. Also a device that circles Earth and transmits information.

savannah: grassland.

scarcity: too little of something.

sediment: bits of rock, sand, or dirt that were carried to a place by water, wind, or a glacier.

sedimentary rock: rock formed from the compression of sediments, the remains of plants and animals, or the evaporation of seawater.

sewage: waste from buildings carried away through sewers.

Siberia: a large, northeastern area of Russia that is isolated and has a cold climate.

smog: fog combined with smoke or other pollutants.

snowmelt: surface runoff produced from melting snow.

snowpack: layers of snow in cold, mountainous areas that remain until warmer weather arrives.

species: a group of living things that have similar characteristics and can produce offspring.

spiral: winding in a continuous and gradually widening or tightening curve.

spore: a single cell that can produce an organism.

staple: an important part of a diet.

storm surge: rising seawater or waves that result from the winds and pressure of a storm.

stratosphere: the layer of Earth's atmosphere above the troposphere, to about 31 miles above Earth, where ozone is found.

strike: an organized protest in which people refuse to work or go to school until changes are made in the workplace or school.

subtropical: an area close to the tropics where the weather is warm.

succulent: a type of plant that has fleshy, thickened parts to retain water that enable it to live in arid climates and soils.

sunny-day flooding: sea water that rises about 2 feet above the typical daily high-tide level.

sustainable: a process or resource that can be used without being completely used up or destroyed.

swamp: an area of wet ground that grows woody plants such as trees and shrubs.

thermal energy: heat energy.

thermal stress: stress that occurs when temperatures become too extreme to handle.

thermosphere: the thickest part of the atmosphere, rising more than 300 miles above the surface of Earth.

tidal station: a geographic location where tidal observations are made.

tide: the daily rise and fall of the ocean's water level near a shore.

topography: the shape of the landscape.

topsoil: the fertile, upper part or layer of soil.

tornado: a violent, twisting, funnel-shaped column of air extending from a thunderstorm to the ground.

transpiration: the process by which plants give off moisture to the atmosphere.

treaty: a formal agreement between two or more countries.

tropical: the hot climate zone to the north and south of the equator.

tropical storm: a storm with wind speeds between 39 and 73 miles per hour.

troposphere: the lowest part of Earth's atmosphere, where most weather occurs.

turbine: a machine that produces energy from moving liquid or air.

typhoon: the name of a hurricane over the western Pacific Ocean.

ultraviolet: invisible energy produced by the sun.

urban: relating to a city or large town.

vector: an organism that transmits a disease from one person to another.

vegetation: all the plant life in a particular area.

virus: a nonliving microbe that can cause disease.

vitamin: an organic molecule that is essential to an organism in small quantities.

vulnerable: exposed to harm.

water cycle: the natural recycling of water through evaporation, condensation, precipitation, and collection.

water vapor: water as a gas, such as fog, steam, or mist.

weather: the temperature, rain, and wind conditions of an area, which change daily.

weather pattern: weather that stays the same for several days or weeks.

wetland: an area where the land is saturated with water. Wetlands are important habitats for fish, plants, and wildlife.

wildfire: a large, destructive fire that spreads out of control.

yield: the amount of a crop harvested on an area of land.

Metric Conversions

Use this chart to find the metric equivalents to the English measurements in this activity. If you need to know a half measurement, divide by two. If you need to know twice the measurement, multiply by two.

English	Metric
1 inch	2.5 centimeters
1 foot	30.5 centimeters
1 yard	0.9 meter
1 mile	1.6 kilometers
1 pound	0.5 kilogram
1 teaspoon	5 milliliters
1 tablespoon	15 milliliters
1 cup	237 milliliters

RESOURCES

BOOKS

Collins, Anna. *The Climate Change Crisis*. Lucent Books, 2018.

Diavolo, Lucy. *No Planet B: A Teen Vogue Guide to the Climate Crisis*. Haymarket Books, 2021.

Heos, Bridget. *It's Getting Hot in Here: The Past, Present, and Future of Climate Change*. Clarion Books, 2016.

Minoglio, Andrea. *Our World Out of Balance: Understanding Climate Change and What We Can Do*. Blue Dot Kids Press, 2021.

Sarah, Rachel. *Girl Warriors: How 25 Young Activists Are Saving the Earth*. Chicago Review Press, 2021.

Sneideman, Josh, and Erin Twamley. *Climate Change: The Science Behind Melting Glaciers and Warming Oceans with Hands-On Science Activities*. Nomad Press, 2020.

Thomas, Keltie. *Rising Seas: Flooding, Climate Change and Our New World*. Firefly Press, 2018.

Neal, Jarrod Shusterman. *Dry*. Simon & Schuster Books for Young Readers, 2018.

Woodward, John. *Climate Change*. DK Publishing, 2021.

WEBSITES

Center for Climate and Energy Solutions
c2es.org

EarthJustice
earthjustice.org

National Geographic
nationalgeographic.com/environment/article/global-warming-overview

National Oceanic and Atmospheric Administration
noaa.gov

Natural Resources Defense Council (NRDC) Climate Change
nrdc.org/issues/climate-change

United Nations Climate Action
un.org/climatechange

U.S. Environmental Protection Agency
epa.gov

U.S. Global Change Research Program
globalchange.gov/climate-change

SELECTED BIBLIOGRAPHY

Abel, David. "Boston already has some of the nation's worst tidal flooding—and it will get much worse, study finds," *The Boston Globe*, July 15, 2020. bostonglobe.com/2020/07/15/metro/boston-has-already-experienced-some-nations-worst-tidal-flooding-its-going-get-much-worse-study-finds

Henson, Robert. *The Thinking Person's Guide to Climate Change*. American Meteorological Society, 2019.

Holden, Emily. "'Like a sunburn on your lungs': How does the climate crisis impact health?" *CBSNews.com*, September 17, 2019. cbsnews.com/news/climate-change-impact-on-health-like-a-sunburn-on-your-lungs

"How Climate Change Is Fueling Extreme Weather." EarthJustice.org, June 1, 2021. earthjustice.org/features/how-climate-change-is-fueling-extreme-weather?gclid=Cj0KCQjwxdSHBhCdARIsAG6zhlWTGOV9lX7LpF_KmBwc1kqg6dqtV9aw3sXgjIO_Y18K8pNtxyC7uqgaAm6jEALw_wcB

Katz, Cheryl. "Small Pests, Big Problems: The Global Spread of Bark Beetles." Yale School of the Environment, September 21, 2017. https://e360.yale.edu/features/small-pests-big-problems-the-global-spread-of-bark-beetles

Quackenbush, Casey. "'A Harbinger of Things to Come': Farmers in Australia Struggle With Its Hottest Drought Ever," *Time*, February 21, 2019. time.com/longform/australia-drought-photos

Romm, Joseph. *Climate Change: What Everyone Needs to Know*. Oxford University Press, 2016.

Welch, Craig. "Half of all Species Are on the Move—And We're Feeling It." *National Geographic*, April 27, 2017. nationalgeographic.com/science/article/climate-change-species-migration-disease

Thunberg, Greta. *No One Is Too Small to Make a Difference*. Penguin Random House, 2019.

Thunberg, Greta. "Our House Is on Fire." World Economic Forum, January 25, 2019, Davos, Switzerland.

RESOURCES

QR CODE GLOSSARY

Page 4: youtube.com/watch?v=M7dVF9xylaw

Page 6: youtube.com/watch?v=e0vj-0imOLw

Page 17: nytimes.com/2021/06/30/world/canada/bc-canada-heat-wave.html

Page 22: tinyurl.com/8ukjay5d

Page 32: wunderground.com

Page 32: weather.gov

Page 32: ncdc.noaa.gov/cdo-web

Page 32: almanac.com/weather/history

Page 37: time.com/longform/australia-drought-photos

Page 39: ucsusa.org/resources/what-sustainable-agriculture?gclid=Cj0KCQjww4OMBhCUARIsAILndv4Hy_2ymRbe0GIP3dGZQsaGQqwHsr2Q5FdO5VxAX9gQKB8DbiBwshAaAr8KEALw_wcB&utm_campaign=food&utm_medium=search&utm_source=googlegrants

Page 42: insideclimatenews.org/news/02052021/extreme-weather-agricultural-financial-risks-climate-change/?gclid=EAIaIQobChMIplSuo7b88QIVASM4Ch0JXQU_EAAYAyAAEgLxXfD_BwE

Page 43: washingtonpost.com/climate-solutions/interactive/2021/saul-griffith-mass-electrification

Page 45: nationalgeographic.com/environment/article/historic-drought-in-west-forcing-ranchers-to-take-painful-measures

Page 52: youtube.com/watch?v=WNpzc3SLkxs&t=19s

Page 63: youtube.com/watch?v=fK8qqvP8Bcc

Page 68: youtube.com/watch?v=dcWIVN02kDQ

Page 71: climate-refugees.org

Page 74: weforum.org/agenda/2021/06/climate-refugees-the-world-s-forgotten-victims

Page 77: npr.org/sections/thetwo-way/2018/03/05/590901652/new-report-predicts-rising-tides-more-flooding

Page 80: youtube.com/watch?v=0QVVzFPChAU&t=18s

Page 84: epa.gov/climate-indicators/climate-change-indicators-sea-level

Page 85: youtube.com/watch?v=rclyP2qDjik

Page 97: health.com/mind-body/cooling-centers-heat-wave

Page 103: youtube.com/watch?v=hvBn8sw3v00

INDEX

M

O

P

R

S

INDEX

T

U

V

W